920 J871c   ~~G401~~   .

Cadenhead, Ivie Edward,
  1923-   23-

Benito Ju´arez

                                             the

world series!

Bibliographical   D0886623

Bibliography: p.179-188.

1. Juárez, Benito Pablo, Pres. Mexico,
1806-1872   I.   Title.   1-10 C

                                              128183

TWAYNE'S
RULERS AND STATESMEN OF THE WORLD
SERIES

Hans L. Trefousse, Brooklyn College
General Editor

BENITO JUÁREZ

(TROW 23)

Benito Juárez

By IVIE E. CADENHEAD, JR.

University of Tulsa

Twayne Publishers, Inc.   ::   New York

ISBN 0-8057-3054-0

MANUFACTURED IN THE UNITED STATES OF AMERICA

To Peggy

To Peggy

Preface

IT SEEMS TO ME FOOLISH TO ATTEMPT TO TELL THE WOULD-BE READER of this book what I have attempted to do here. It is obviously an effort to recount in a relatively short space the major aspects of the life and times of Benito Juárez, a man who no one would deny deserves treatment as a true "statesman of the world." The problems of biography are obvious to all who have written or read one, and they are multiplied by any effort to be concise. I can only hope that I have touched upon the most important facts, made as few errors of fact and interpretation as is humanly possible and helped to create an admiration for a man's accomplishments without overlooking his failings.

Any statement of indebtedness would have to include the staffs of the various libraries referred to in the bibliography with a special note of thanks to the University of Tulsa Library for assistance and cooperation in the search for primary and secondary materials. Mrs. Mary Lou Baker, as she has so often, typed the manuscript with care and without complaint. I am also indebted to the University of Tulsa Faculty Research Program for a grant that made possible a trip to Mexico, and to the Oklahoma Consortium on Research Development for a matching grant that allowed the acquisition of materials otherwise not available. Finally, I am especially indebted to the University of Tulsa for allowing me a sabbatical leave in Mexico to do research and writing and, most of all, absorb something of the feel of the nation of Juárez— a feeling I hope comes through in this book.

IVIE E. CADENHEAD, JR.

Cuernavaca, Mexico, and Tulsa, Oklahoma
1972, "The Year of Juárez"

Contents

Contents

Chronology

1806   Born in San Paulo Guelatao.
1818   Moves to city of Oaxaca.
1821–1828   Enters seminary and studies for priesthood.
1828   Begins study of law in the Institute.
1829   Serves as lieutenant in militia.
1830–1841   Teaches physics and later law at the Institute.
1830   Begins practice of law.
1831   Elected to city council.
1832   Elected to state legislature.
1833   Named aide to General Isidro Reyes.
1834   Formally admitted to the bar and named acting judge.
1841   Appointed judge.
1843   Marries Margarita Maza.
1844   Becomes secretary of cabinet under Governor León.
1845   Elected to Departmental Assembly.
1846   Serves as member of temporary triumvirate governing the state and then becomes chief justice.
1846–1847   Serves as delegate to national congress.
1847   Elected governor *pro-tempore*.
1848   Elected to full term as governor.
1852   Named Director of Institute of Sciences and Art.
1853   Arrested by Santanistas and goes into exile in New Orleans.
1855   Returns to Acapulco and joins the Alvarez government.
1855   Resumes post as governor of Oaxaca under Comonfort appointment.
1857   Elected governor under Constitution of 1857.
1857   Appointed Secretary of *Gobernación*.
1858   Assumes presidency upon departure of Comonfort.
1858–1861   Leads nation during War of the Reform.
1859   Issues new Reform Laws.
1861   Returns to Mexico City at end of War of the Reform.

1861 Elected president.
1862–1867 Leads Mexico against French Intervention.
1863 Moves government to San Luis Potosí.
1864 Moves government to Saltillo, then Monterrey, and finally Chihuahua.
1865 Prolongs term in office.
1867 Victorious over Maximilian; returns to Mexico City.
1867 Issues *convocatoria.*
1867 Reelected president.
1869–1870 Faces rebellions and congressional opposition.
1870 Suffers stroke.
1871 Wife dies.
1871 Runs again for reelection and wins.
1871–1872 Faces rebellion of Porfirio Díaz.
1872 Dies after a series of heart attacks.

CHAPTER I

Early Life

"AT THAT TIME, GREAT EVENTS HAD ALREADY OCCURRED IN THE NA-
tion."[1] Thus, Benito Juárez began a brief summary of the events
of the Mexican nation prior to his own public life. Indeed, great
events had taken place during the first two decades of the nineteenth century, but the seeds of the fortunes and misfortunes of
the Mexican people had been sown long before in the policies of
imperial Spain toward her colonies, if not in the practices of the
Aztec conquerors who preceded them.

For almost three centuries Spanish rule imposed upon the
people of New Spain the rules, institutions, and habits that were
to plague the new nation of Mexico, as well as provide a base on
which to build. True, there were brief interruptions in Spanish
control because of distance from Spain or, in the case of Charles
III (1759–1788), an enlightened ruler, but overall the Spanish
word was law and was carried out through a well-developed viceregal system dominated by the *gachupines,* those of pure Spanish
blood lucky enough to have been born in Spain. The end result
was the development of a variety of discontented elements in the
colony, having little else in common besides their discontent. The
criollo, just as Spanish in ancestry as the *gachupin* but born in
the New World, grew increasingly resentful of his secondary role.
He saw positions in government, both civil and ecclesiastical, in
the military and the professions either closed to him or limited in
their availability. The *mestizo,* frequently the result of casual
union between Spaniard and Indian, found himself even further
down the social and economic ladder, unclaimed by his father
and unacceptable to his mother's people or unwilling to identify
himself with those whose lot was even worse than his own. The
Indians, who had been decimated by the near genocide of the con-
quest and whose land had been taken by the Spaniards, had been
reduced to a status little better than slavery.

[13]

In addition to the evils attributable to the pernicious system of *casta*, Spanish mercantile policy contributed to a general decline of the economy. Spain, like other nations with colonial empires, looked upon her colonies as areas to be exploited. This meant severe restrictions upon trade and the development of local industry as well as upon certain types of agriculture; a multitude of taxes either directly or indirectly imposed upon the colonials themselves; and an almost complete inability to understand the complaints from the colonies.

While the ideas associated with the French Enlightenment reached only a few in the New World, it was perhaps inevitable that the serious questioning of the established order would find a few willing ears in Mexico and this, in turn, would produce activity aimed at least at reform of the Spanish system. The process was indirect, to be sure, and a straight-line connection between European ideas and the coming of independence is difficult to demonstrate. Yet there was, by the late colonial period, artistic and intellectual activity in Mexico that influenced the years ahead. Schools were established; greater attention was given to the scientific discoveries of Europe; scientific mining methods were introduced, and newspapers, literary journals, and papers dedicated to archeolchy, anthropolgy, and science were published. All of this led to a general critical spirit, a questioning of established institutions. Arguments on behalf of free trade, the reduction of special privileges for older ruling classes, not to mention debates concerning the rights of monarchs and the all-pervasive influence of the Catholic church, had their effect.

Especially important for the political and economic future of Mexico were changes made in the administrative structure of New Spain during the late 1760s and early 1770s. José de Gálvez, originally a royal investigator and later Minister of the Indies, was instrumental in creating a more autonomous subdivision of government for the Interior Provinces, a region stretching from Durango north to Santa Fé. The problems of this region were different from those of Mexico City, Guadalajara, and Veracruz, but until Gálvez's survey taxes paid by this northern region were spent primarily in Mexico City. Future Mexican governments would be plagued with the same regional desires and jealousies.

Similarly, the Spanish trade reforms of the eighteenth century aroused hopes on the part of ports other than Veracruz and the areas they served that a true free-port system might be established. Those areas favored by Spanish policy or by geographic advantage naturally feared competition. Here again issues of regionalism created by Spanish policy were to be a part of the inheritance of a Mexican nation.[2]

The Napoleonic invasion of Spain in 1808 and the enforced "visit" of Ferdinand VII to France produced a series of confusions that allowed reactions throughout Spanish America. In several of the colonies *criollo* governments took over in the name of Ferdinand and *de facto* independence resulted. In other colonies *criollo* rule succeeded for a time only to have Spanish authority reestablished and independence subsequently fought for.

Mexico had its own unique history. In Mexico City, the dominant *gachupines* successfully headed off attempts by *criollos* to assume the sovereignty they felt the absence of a Spanish monarch gave them. Plots and counterplots were essayed in most of the major cities but only in Valladolid, in 1809, was a serious effort made to effect a revolution against the authorities in Mexico City. This move was apparently designed only to put the *criollos* in control rather than bring about independence, and it met an inglorious end. Meanwhile, a then insignificant parish priest, Miguel Hidalgo y Costilla, in the small village of Dolores had been meeting and planning revolt with a handful of others. They envisioned an uprising of mistreated Indians and underprivileged *mestizos* led by resentful *criollos* slowly developing and ultimately challenging *gachupin* authority in New Spain.

This dangerous plan could hardly escape detection, however, and well before the December, 1810, date set for action, royal officials ordered a round-up of the known conspirators. Thus it was that the men of Dolores were called out by the ringing of the church bell and Hidalgo delivered an inspiring preachment on the political doctrine of independence. He concluded by calling upon his parishioners to take up arms to achieve independence and to kill the Spaniards. This "grito de Dolores" converted a reform movement aimed at *criollo* power with little or no change in the basic economic and social structure of the country into an Indian and *mestizo* uprising too turbulent for the esteemed father to control.

Throughout the countryside the people armed themselves with machetes, bows and arrows, guns, any weapons available and joined the ranks of the army now marching under the banner of the Virgin of Guadalupe. A bloodbath at Guanajuato was followed by murder and rampant destruction at Guadalajara and other locations invested by the unleashed fury of the submerged classes. Their atrocities were met in kind by conservative armies defending the power of the viceregal authority. The monster that Hidalgo had created appalled him and kept away from his revolution many of the *criollos* upon whom it had depended—or those who had joined defected as the racial aspects of the movement became more apparent. By mid-1811 Hidalgo's hopes of success had faded and, as the result of traitorous support, Hidalgo and other leaders were captured and executed.

The cause of the masses was not completely obliterated, however. One of Hidalgo's students from an earlier time, also a parish priest but a *mestizo*, took up the banner of Hidalgo. José María Morelos y Pavón planned a slower, more deliberate, and more profound revolution. He fought not only for the independence of the Mexican nation as had Hidalgo, but also for legal and social reform that touched upon the great problems of land ownership, governmental participation, the caste system, and the excesses of wealth and power of the *gachupín* bishops. Unfortunately, the *criollo* disenchantment with Hidalgo's revolt carried over to help defeat Morelos's vision of a Mexican nation. He too was captured and executed in late 1815 and an end had almost come to any organized revolutionary movement. Minor revolutionary bands continued to harass the royalists but they were gradually defeated, broken up, or driven into the hills or forests where resistance was possible in little more than name. Two such steadfast proponents of continuing the fight were Guadalupe Victoria, known generally as Félix Fernández before adopting that pseudonym, and Vicente Guerrero. Victoria, a *criollo*, wandered for two years in the region between Puebla and Veracruz awaiting the day when he could assist in achieving the independence of his nation. Guerrero, a *mestizo*, kept a small band of insurgents operating in the Sierra Madre del Sur with arms and supplies captured from royalist armies. Ironically, though Guerrero was to be allowed to participate in the ultimate decision for independence, the movement he led was to be corrupted and he, himself, was to be deceived in its achievement.

The true initiative for a successful declaration of independence came from the very elements that had crushed Hidalgo and Morelos. Early in 1820, a liberal uprising forced Ferdinand VII of Spain to accept a constitution written in 1812 by the then regency of Spain ruling in his name and opposing the forces of Napoleon. After the defeat of Napoleon, Ferdinand had returned to power, thrown out the limited monarchy called for by the constitution, and set about reestablishing his autocratic power in Spain as well as its colonies. The spirit and ideal of the Enlightenment had carried too far, however, for the Spanish people to allow the complete restoration of the past monarchy. Their liberalism, grounded in freedom of speech and press as well as a degree of anti-clericalism, was anathema to conservative elements in Mexico. Members of the higher clergy in Mexico, having excommunicated Hidalgo, Morelos, Guerrero, and others for ideas only a little more offensive than those being spread in Spain, set about to protect their own land from such an insidious movement.

Convincing the Viceroy that Guerrero must be destroyed, spokesmen for the episcopate suggested that one Agustín de Iturbide be given command of royalist troops to achieve that result. Iturbide, a *criollo* and former royalist officer, had earlier been deprived of his army position for a somewhat too zealous seizure of money from those within his military district—and for pocketing most of it himself. In an effort to recoup his position, Iturbide had ingratiated himself with members of the higher clergy and convinced them that he was a man with sufficient military skill, imagination, and loyalty to carry out the job of defeating Guerrero.

For a number of days Iturbide marched and countermarched but was never able to subdue Guerrero or even make contact with his main forces. He then, as perhaps he had always planned, offered Guerrero his own alliance in the cause of independence. Guerrero, though naturally suspicious, was finally convinced of Iturbide's sincerity and issued along with Iturbide the Plan of the Three Guarantees at Iguala. This agreement established an independent Mexico under a still-to-be-selected European monarch with equality for all Mexicans. Victoria came out of his mountain fastness and with other former partisans of the cause of Morelos gave his backing to the Plan of Iguala. *Criollos,* less afraid of this non-Indianist movement and anxious to acquire the freedoms that independence seemed to offer, gave their support to the cause of the trigarantine army. The Viceroy, virtually unsupported, did what he could to oppose the rebel move but independence was achieved with virtually no bloodshed and with little tremor to the status quo.

Though Iturbide marched into Mexico City on September 27, 1821, with Guerrero and Victoria at his side, the independence that had been achieved had little resemblance to that envisioned earlier by Morelos. The old economic and social order remained almost unaltered. Class distinctions were not relaxed and the army and clergy retained their *fueros* or special privileges. In addition, within weeks after establishing independence, the wily Iturbide gave in to the "demands" of his own troops and accepted the throne of Mexico as Agustín I. All the Spaniards who could left Mexico, taking with them their wealth. *Criollo* conservatives assumed the positions of political and ecclesiastical power that had been vacated and hoped for the opportunity to replace one exploiting class with another. It took very little time for the Indians and *mestizos,* who had seen Iguala as the consummation of a dream, to discover that nothing had changed for them. Indeed, the destruction and indebtedness caused by the wars between 1810 and 1821 coupled with the loss of Spanish support produced economic conditions in the new nation even worse than those of colonial times. Mines had gone unworked and some never reopened. Fields had gone unharvested and cattle uncared for. Trade was disrupted and this would reduce still further Mexico's uncertain ability to borrow money abroad at anything resembling advantageous rates.

For the next thirty years there were many disturbances, but not genuine revolution, unless the overthrow of Iturbide in 1823 and the establishment of a republican system of government under the Constitution of 1824 can be so considered. The conflicts that continued under the republic appeared to revolve around the question of whether the national government was to be organized as a federal or a unitary system. The centralist party attracted most of the conservatives, the landowning class, the military, and the clergy, while federalism appealed to the *mestizos,* who still desired opportunities in politics, and to a growing liberal faction composed of men of all classes who wished to subordinate the church and the army to the civil authorities.

Emerging out of these decades of conflict and taking advantage of the confusion was the overpowering figure of Antonio López de Santa Anna. An opportunistic *caudillo,* Santa Anna was to change his politics with each shift of the wind and emerge ultimately as the supreme dictator toward which he had always tended. Yet, his influence for better or worse was to give to an era of Mexican history the label the Age of Santa Anna.

In spite of the tides that rose and fell and the preeminence of Santa Anna, an occasional portent of things to come could be seen. The radicals, or at least the more radical element of the liberal faction, gained control of the government for a few months in 1833–34 under Valentín Gómez Farías, a Zacatecan physician and devoted liberal, who oddly enough enjoyed power only because Santa Anna had established him in the vice-presidency and had retired to his plantation to await events. Nonetheless, an imposing series of reforms was enacted in a brief period. Payment of tithes was no longer compulsory; religious oaths could be retracted; public education was completely secularized; the clerical University of Mexico was suppressed; the right of patronage was transferred to the state; and the secularization of church property was begun. In addition, the army was reduced in size and its officers deprived of their *fueros.*

The mass of the people, apparently not realizing what the struggle was about and certainly not identifying it with the plans of Father Morelos, simply followed the habits of a lifetime and rallied around the clergy and military when called upon to bring an end to this incipient liberal movement. The conservatives were returned to power but a continuity between the dreams of 1810 and the events of the future had been established. Any young man beginning a political career in the 1830s would have been forced to face the choices for the future and, if he had ideals and convictions, begin to fight for them.

Looking back across a span of thirty-six years to the date of independence, Benito Juárez could indeed reflect that great events had taken place. The truth is, however, that much of his knowledge of those events was second-hand and he can even be forgiven for capsuling the history even more than has been done here. The fact that he overlooked as significant a figure as Morelos in his account is more an indication of his effort to simply summarize the events and attitudes of which he was most aware in 1857 than of any conscious desire to slight one of the important figures in the period of the fight for independence.[3] At the time he composed his notes for his children he was more concerned with the nation he would hopefully leave to them than with detailing what had transpired before his own time.

Benito Pablo Juárez was born only four years before the Grito de Dolores, on March 21, 1806, in San Paulo Guelatao in the state of Oaxaca, a village of scarcely twenty families. His parents were full-blooded Zapotec Indians who dutifully and in all probability sincerely arranged for their son's baptism on the day following his birth.[4] After all, it would not have been unusual in that time and place for the child to have died within hours after his birth. Evidence is scanty, but it is reasonable to assume that Juárez's parents were little different from hundreds, if not thousands, of Indian couples living in small villages, raising children, attending church, and struggling for survival in late colonial Mexico. It is known that Marcelino Juárez, the father, and Brígida García, the mother, both died when their son was barely three years old.

After the death of his parents, Juárez was cared for by his paternal grandparents until their death, at which time an uncle, Bernardino Juárez, assumed responsibility for the young boy. Two sisters had already married and moved away from the village of their birth, one of them ultimately to the city of Oaxaca, a fact that was to have importance in Juárez's future. For several years, however, Juárez stayed in San Paulo Guelatao, working for and with his uncle and engaging in what were probably typical activities for a young boy in a small Indian village. It appears that Juárez remembered his uncle as a stern, even hard, man, but a man who produced in his ward an understanding of the importance of education—at least the ability to understand the Spanish language—and probably first planted in Juárez's mind the idea of becoming a priest.[5] Such a career, though hardly a pinnacle of worldly success, at least offered to the poor Indian of Mexico a measure of escape from an otherwise highly uncertain existence.

Juárez felt keenly the security that living with his uncle in familiar surroundings gave him, and he had the usual circle of childhood friends whose loss it would be difficult to replace. Yet, the possibility of moving to Oaxaca was obviously present. "The struggle that existed between these sentiments," he wrote, "and my desire to go to another society, new and unknown to me, in

order to obtain my education, was cruel." By December, 1818, the
lure of the city and its opportunities finally became too much for
the twelve-year-old boy in the mountains above Oaxaca. Ambition and the belief that only in the city could he get the education he had not been able to get at home, won out.[6] Without a
word to his uncle, who might have prevented it, he made his
departure, walking the almost forty miles to the city where he
sought the aid of his sister María Josefa.

María was employed as a cook in the home of a small business-
man, Antonio Maza, a kindly Italian known to his neighbors as
El Gachupín because they thought him Spanish. Maza, hardly
anticipating the assistance he was giving his adopted country or
the close ties of family that would result, generously gave
Juárez a home for a few weeks and odd jobs that paid him two
reales a day until he was able to make a more permanent and
suitable arrangement.[7]

On January 7, 1819, possibly with the help of Maza or María,
Juárez was taken into the home of Don Antonio Salanueva, a
pious bookbinder who was a member of the Third Order of St.
Francis and a reasonably well-read and liberal man. Under the
apparent kindly and generous direction of Salanueva, Juárez
entered the equivalent of the city schools of Oaxaca. Though
he transferred from his first school to another, the Royal School,
Juárez soon discovered that caste distinctions did indeed exist
and his lack of knowledge of Spanish was an almost insuperable
handicap, given the methods of instruction and lack of consideration by most of the instructors. Thus, he elected to quit
school and practice on his own as much as he had been able to
learn. With perseverance, with the advantages of his god-
father's library, and probably assistance from friendly neighbors,
Juárez was able to achieve an acceptable, if informal, fluency
in Spanish. That he was remembered as always having a book
in his hand is both a sign of his diligence and also of his success in obtaining books from a variety of sources.[8]

Though the young Zapotec's education already exceeded
that of most of his peers at the time, the memory of his uncle's
suggestion that he enter the priesthood lingered on. The atmosphere of Oaxaca, as perhaps all of Mexico, made the church
and religion the center of all life. To become a priest was a
dream held by many. There was in Oaxaca a seminary, Semi-

nario Conciliar de la Cruz, whose students Juárez had observed, and he had become aware that they were held in high respect for the knowledge they were assumed to have. Discussion with Don Antonio produced the fact that Juárez's knowledge of the Zapotec language and his Indian blood would allow him to enter the seminary without the usual patrimony to get him started. Thus, in October, 1821, he began the study for the priesthood. It was only eight months after the issuance of the Plan of Iguala and less than one month since Iturbide's triumphal entry into Mexico City. To the student of Oaxaca, his personal trials and decisions were still largely unrelated to the affairs of his new nation. Indeed, the fact of independence had, as yet, little direct effect on Juárez's life.

For almost seven years Juárez painfully endured the training offered by the seminary, struggling with Latin grammar when he knew not even Spanish grammar and maneuvering his curriculum so as to add courses in the arts before completing his training in moral philosophy, the last step toward his career as a priest. In spite of obvious handicaps, Juárez did quite well at his studies and acquired a good if limited and impractical knowledge of the subjects available to a seminary student.[9] We cannot be certain, even after reading Juárez's own reminiscences, that he knew that a priestly life was not his real choice for the future. True, with the advantage of hindsight, he recalled an "instinctive repugnance" for the priesthood even when he entered the seminary. It is clear, however, that until 1827 there was no real alternative for a young man of his status other than the military, a career he also was to find distasteful. In 1827, though, the effects of the establishment of a Mexican republic with some semblance of liberalism were felt in Oaxaca and changed the situation slightly. The most direct effect, so far as Juárez's life was concerned, was the creation by a newly-elected state legislature of a civil college, the Institute of Sciences and Arts, a school independent of the church and designed to provide a somewhat broader curriculum than the traditional clerical variety.[10]

Since the new road to education seemed to offer at least the opportunity to enter law and medicine, numerous students immediately transferred from the seminary. Juárez stayed on for the last year of instruction in theology, partly to please Don

Antonio, but in 1828 he entered the Institute to begin the study of law. These studies and the almost natural involvement in politics that they produced marked the beginning of a career for Juárez that would lead him into the center of those great events shaping his nation. It is highly doubtful if anyone, even Juárez himself, could have anticipated the heights to which he would rise, but it would soon become clear that he was a man to be reckoned with at least within the narrow horizons of the city and state of Oaxaca.

CHAPTER II

Emergence as a National Figure

THE NEW INSTITUTE IN WHICH JUÁREZ WAS NOW A STUDENT PRO-
vided less of an experience of students learning from teachers
than of a mutual educational process. The limitations of education in the past meant that the professors were only a little
ahead of their students and frequently even called upon those
students who demonstrated unusual ability in a subject to help
teach it. In addition, the Institute was under constant attack
from the local clergy and their conservative allies, a fact which
delayed its growth. Though the director, Francisco Aparicio,
and several of the staff were priests themselves and hardly anticlerical, the faculty was liberal on political issues and was considered a threat to the influence and power of the church.[1] Aparicio had been a friend of Morelos and strongly pro-independ-
ence and others on the staff were perhaps considered even more
radical for the time.[2] Thus, though the school was to produce in
time two presidents, six ministers of state, and a number of
lesser public figures, the attrition of students at the beginning
was high partly because of the opposition that developed as
well as the normal reasons for students dropping out: lack of
funds, lack of ability, or loss of motivation.[3] Juárez stuck with
his plans, however, and found the almost innate liberalism
produced by his Indian background and personal struggles reinforced by those who instructed him.[4]

It should not be concluded, however, that Juárez was developing any truly original ideas about government or even ideas
that were necessarily practical in the existing Mexican situation.
The number of books available to him was naturally limited
and even his strongest supporters were unlikely to regard him
as an intellectual. Juárez, like all individuals, passed through
formative years and would have found it difficult to determine

exactly what influences were most directly responsible for his later beliefs and actions.

Indicative, perhaps, of the young student's limited political awareness was his failure to record in much detail the significant events taking place during his law school years in Oaxaca, as well as the nation, when he composed his notes for his children in later life. In 1828, the very year that Juárez entered the Institute, presidential elections took place under the federal constitution of 1824. Since Guadalupe Victoria, the incumbent, could not run for reelection, two candidates wanted to succeed him: Vicente Guerrero, champion of the federalist cause, and Manuel Gómez Pedraza, former Minister of War and candidate of those favoring a centralist form of government. The results of the election indicated that Gómez Pedraza had won, but there were those leaders who refused to accept a result that they believed to be unrepresentative of the people's wishes. The outcome was military action against the government.

Among the first to pronounce against Gómez Pedraza was Santa Anna. A former royalist officer, Santa Anna had joined the cause of independence and had been reasonably consistent in his loyalty to Victoria and now Guerrero. His pronouncement, carefully timed to occur on September 11, 1828, the anniversary of Father Hidalgo's "Grito de Dolores," failed however to attract immediate or substantial support. As a result, Santa Anna fled from the fortress of San Carlos de Perote, which he had seized, with his small force of eight hundred men southward to Oaxaca. Though he seized the city, he was immediately besieged by forces loyal to Gómez Pedraza and might well have lost all had not others joined in support of his initial movement. Juan Álvarez, long a supporter of freedom from his stronghold in the west, revolted in Mexico City on November 30. With the success of the rebellion assured, the siege of Oaxaca was lifted and Santa Anna received appropriate rewards from Guerrero.

Before he left for Veracruz, however, Santa Anna, for his success in Oaxaca, was honored with a special dinner by a professor at the Institute. Santa Anna was later to recall meeting a barefoot Indian by the name of Benito Juárez who waited on his table. Though the story might be apocryphal, it is quite possible that the meeting did take place. Even if it did not, Juárez's failure to recall Santa Anna's presence in Oaxaca during those fateful days is significant.[5]

Perhaps Juárez simply failed to comment upon these events in his recollections or, equally possible, the continuation and successful conclusion of his law studies were more to be remembered in recalling his personal career. Surely he, like other liberals, supported Guerrero, the great successor to Morelos, but found there was no opportunity to contribute personally to his cause.[6] Certainly he was making progress in his chosen field. By 1830 he was substituting as a teacher of physics at the Institute and apparently had achieved enough income to have left the home of Salanueva. Within a year he had passed his examinations and begun the practice of law in the office of Don Tiburcio Cañas. He had also begun a political career with his election as an alderman of the city council of Oaxaca. Equally important to him, however, was his continued work at the Institute as Secretary and as a teacher of physics.[7] The memory that one of his students successfully defended his thesis before the faculty of the Institute was equal in importance to his first successful election. The teaching of science and the practice of law were not only equally important but not at all incompatible.

The first of only two direct exposures to military life had come during his last years in law school. In 1828, the Spanish, hoping to take advantage of the internal upheaval in Mexico, dispatched troops from Cuba and seized the port of Tampico. Rumors and fears of an imminent Spanish attack led to the calling out of a civil militia in Oaxaca to prepare for the defense of the city. Juárez modestly admits that he was named a lieutenant, but there is no reason to believe that he engaged in any combat, and the appointment was a short one since the Spanish were driven out primarily by yellow fever and secondarily by Mexican forces.

Events on the larger stage of national politics continued to intrude upon the limited confines of the new Oaxacan lawyer and teacher. In late 1829, the Vice-President, Anastasio Bustamante, fearful of the loss of privileges for himself and his military colleagues, threw Guerrero out of office. Guerrero, though a social and political liberal, had supported the monopoly of Catholicism in Mexico, and by implication at least had represented no serious threat to the established order. However, his overthrow more strongly drew the lines between contending factions, and liberals began a fight to restore Guerrero to the presidency. Though the liberals triumphed by 1833, Guerrero had already been tricked into capture in 1831. His alleged trial was held in Oaxaca and he was taken to the Dominican convent at Cuilapam a few miles outside the city where he was shot. This action, coupled with the general disrepute of the Bustamante government, brought others to the federalist side, including the inevitable Santa Anna.

Juárez must have been aware of the overthrow of Guerrero and his trial in Oaxaca and it is also reasonable to suppose that he, like all those who venerated Guerrero for his part in the coming of independence, was appalled at the circumstances. Unfortunately, Juárez's autobiographical recollection continues with a comment on the revolt against Bustamante and records only bare facts about succeeding presidents. Perhaps this is just as well, for the exact sequence of events is one of those complex sets of personal, political, ideological, and circumstantial conflicts that frequently characterize Mexico in the nineteenth century. Valentín Gómez Farías, a staunch liberal, issued the famous Plan of Zacatecas and joined with other leaders already in revolt in the north and west to support the overthrow of Bustamante and the return of Gómez Pedraza, who had been constitutionally elected to the presidency in 1828. Santa Anna was quick to support this plan and provided the primary military leadership that brought it success. Thus it was arranged that Gómez Pedraza serve as interim president from December 21, 1832, until April 1, 1833. Meanwhile, a presidential election was held and the results announced in March showed that Santa Anna had received the votes of sixteen of eighteen state legislatures for the presidency with Gómez Farías elected vice-president, having received the vote of eleven states. Apparently a liberal, federal regime had been instituted. Santa Anna retired to his estate at Manga de Clavo, not even bothering to go to Mexico City to take the oath of office. Instead, he turned the direction of the government over to his vice-president who was to oversee the anticipated reforms.

In Oaxaca, as well as in Mexico City, the liberals took over the government with consequent effects on the life of Juárez. In Oaxaca he was elected one of the members of the new state legislature, a position he held for only a short time and for which no record of significant contribution remains. He did introduce one measure designed to have Guerrero's remains declared the property of the state and to have a proper sepulcher built, a sufficiently liberal action to give Juárez a bad name in the minds of local conservatives.[8] Another effect of the liberal victory on Juárez stemmed from the passage by the federal government of a law calling for the expulsion of certain Spaniards, including a number of bishops. The time had come when Juárez could have been officially ordained a priest, but without a bishop this was impossible and whatever remaining hopes Don Antonio had had that his former ward would follow a clerical career were dashed and he gave his consent for him to continue the practice of law.

The fact that military and clerical opponents of the reforms of Gómez Farías were in a constant state of revolt against the government from the time he took office until the end of 1834, also influenced the life of Juárez. One such revolt broke out in Oaxaca in 1833, when forces under the conservative General Valentín Canalizo attacked the city. Juárez was named aide to the defending General, Isidro Reyes, and, since at least a part of the city was taken by Canalizo, probably engaged in the street fighting that took place before the conservatives were driven out.

The victory in Oaxaca, like others, was in vain, however, because the liberals remained in power only a few months, and their overthrow at the national level would again cause changes at the local level. Early in January, 1834, Juárez was formally admitted to the bar and a few days later was named an acting judge, a post he held for only a few months. The briefness of his tenure was related to the fact that Santa Anna, after considerable vacillation, in December, 1834, assumed his presidency, threw out the anticlerical laws and exiled his own vice-president.[9] Liberal members of local and state governments immediately fell from power. Juárez was confined for a time in the city of Tehuacán; whether he was confined to a single house or to the city limits is unclear. In any event, he had now tasted personally the fate of a loser in the political struggle.

Upon his return to the practice of law Juárez seemed unable or unwilling to avoid taking the side of liberalism against the reestablished clerical-military rule. On at least one occasion he was obliged to spend nine days in jail because of a case he had undertaken against a parish priest who he felt had charged unjustly high fees. This experience contributed to his conclusion that:

These blows that I suffered, and that almost daily I saw suffered by the unprotected who complained of the arbitrary acts of the privileged classes in close association with the civil authority, showed me most clearly that society would never be happy while those classes existed in alliance with the public powers, and confirmed me in my resolution to work unceasingly to destroy the evil power of the privileged classes.[10]

Along with the continued practice of law, Juárez remained associated with the Institute, now teaching civil and canon law. In 1841 he was again appointed to a judgeship, perhaps in the aftermath of another attempt by liberals to overthrow the conservative rule of then President Bustamante. Not all of Juárez's activity was entirely legal or academic during these years. At least one of his biographers, and there is supporting evidence, maintains that he fathered two illegitimate children, Tereso and Susana. The fate of Tereso is unknown, but Susana later became an invalid and a narcotics addict and was cared for by friends of Juárez, who seems to have felt a genuine concern for his child.[11]

Such illicit liaisons were at least to be limited in the future, because on July 31, 1843, Juárez married Doña Margarita Maza, the seventeen-year-old daughter of the family for whom his sister had worked and in whose home he had stayed on his arrival in Oaxaca many years before. The marriage took place in the church of San Felipe Neri in Oaxaca. It made official the long close relationship of Juárez with the Maza family and in time produced twelve children. There were nine daughters: Manuela, Margarita, Felícitas, Soledad, María de Jesús, María Josefa, Amada, Francisca, and Guadalupe; and three sons: Benito, José, and Antonio. The new Señora Juárez is known to have remarked of her husband only that, "He is very homely but very good."[12] Perhaps that and the evidence of twelve children is enough to conclude that a long and happy marriage had begun.

During the early years of the 1840s it appeared that Juárez had lost, or at least compromised, whatever reforming zeal he may have had. Out of the stream of national politics, he can be viewed as simply another middle-aged man who had assumed the responsibilities of a family and was concerned only with making a living and adjusting to whatever political winds might blow through his home state. Certainly, his appointment by a conservative governor, General don Antonio León, as secretary of the cabinet in 1844 makes it appear that his liberalism was well concealed.[13] Moreover, when a new and more centralized national government was shortly instituted, Juárez was appointed Second Prosecutor of his newly-created Department.

Defenders of Juárez's reputation during this period, however, point out that, by working with a Santanista governor, he was able to influence state policy in a variety of ways.[14] He was at least partially responsible for reform of the court system, for the beginning of some much-needed road and railroad construction, for improvements in state health services, and encouraging the introduction of new crops to broaden the state's agricultural base.[15] It is also true that he finally resigned from his post with the cabinet after a disagreement with Governor León.[16] Clearly his influence was little diminished at the time because he was unanimously elected to be a member of the new Departmental Assembly, or state legislature, in 1845.

It is also clear that Juárez had become an ardent worker in the Rito Nacional Mexicano by this time, obtaining the highest rank in this successor to the Yorkinos, or York Rite Masons. Though this later organization had less apparent political significance than had the Masonic movement at the time of independence, it still represented opposition to centralistic tendencies in government and supported pro-republican ideals as well as anticlerical views. Juárez's identification with the Rito Nacional indicates his continued association with others in Oaxaca whose liberalism was seldom called into question and suggests that he had no difficulty in identifying himself with men of such convictions.[17]

It may be that Juárez's apparent ideological inconsistencies can be explained by a very simple fact—the history of his country at the time. For during the 1830s and 1840s the Mexican nation's own direction was far from clear. Contending federalist and centralist factions alternated in power with discouraging frequency and the opportunistic Santa Anna added his own personal ambitions to the confusion. If this tendency toward national suicide were not enough, Mexico faced foreign enemies as well, not just the traditional threat from Spain but French harassment and the overwhelming threat from the colossus to the north, the United States.

Santa Anna's return to the presidency in 1834 had not brought stability to the government. True, the centralists had been returned to power but Santa Anna was as unpredictable as ever. Once again pleading illness, he had turned the direction of the nation over to Miguel Barragán as interim president and then retired to his hacienda. Under Barragán a new constitution, known as "Las siete leyes," was drafted in 1836 and the way paved for a truly centralistic dictatorship. Obviously, Federalists throughout the nation objected and in several areas took up arms. The most important opposition, as it turned out, came from Texas where federalist resistance to a centralist regime was to develop into a war for Texan independence.

The story of the troubles in Texas is too long to be told here. Suffice it to say that in the years after Stephen F. Austin led a group of settlers into northern Mexico under Mexican encouragement, significant differences had developed between the English-speaking, Protestant Americans, some of them slaveowners, and the Spanish-speaking, Catholic Mexican authorities of the state of Coahuila of which they were a part. These differences made Americans in Texas natural allies of Federalists throughout the nation. The events of 1834 and 1835 convinced Texans, however, including some of Mexican birth, that their struggle for autonomy and self-government was doomed to failure, and on November 3, 1835, the fight was officially declared one for independence.

Santa Anna chose this moment to come out of retirement and engage in the activity with which he was best identified, that of a military leader. As it turned out, his campaign against Texas failed and resulted in his being discredited at home. Though he won a bloody victory at the Alamo, a surprise attack by Sam Houston at San Jacinto resulted in the destruction of Santa Anna's army and his own ultimate capture. Defeat he might have survived but when it became known to his countrymen that Santa Anna was willing to barter away Texas for his own life, his political future seemed over. Yet, within a brief eighteen months he was a national hero again. In April, 1838, the French established a naval blockade at Veracruz as part of a debt collection move. What followed is known as "The Pastry War" since one of the claims involved a French pastry cook. Santa Anna was called to assist in the defense of the city and in the fighting that followed suffered a wound that led to the amputation of his leg. For a time it appeared that he might even lose his life.

Not only did Santa Anna not die but within three months he was operating as a military commander from a litter, supporting the then-president Bustamante against federalist forces.[18] Two years had not passed before he officially denounced Bustamante, defeated him, and on October 10, 1841, for the third time was installed in the presidency.[19] Santa Anna actually served in the office for three years this time and some of his supporters in the various states lasted even longer. This was the period of the governorship of León in Oaxaca and Juárez's association with him. In December, 1844, however, Santa Anna was himself overthrown and for a year the weak and ineffectual José Joaquín de Herrera attempted to hold a government together. A military uprising led by General Mariano Paredes y Anelloga ended his hopes.[20] On January 2, 1846, Paredes was installed in Mexico City as temporary dictator only to face a confused Congress, dissident Federalists, and the threat of war with the United States.

This confusing kaleidoscope of events had its repercussions in Oaxaca and upon the career of Benito Juárez; no one, however, could have even yet foretold the future importance of the Assemblyman in Oaxaca. The most immediate result of the takeover by Paredes was the loss of another position by Juárez because the Departmental Assembly, scarcely a year old, was dissolved. Opposition to Paredes developed in Oaxaca as elsewhere, led in this instance by General Juan Bautista Díaz. The movement was successful nationwide; Paredes was removed and on August 6 was replaced by José Mariano Salas as acting president. In Oaxaca, five days later, a Committee of Notables named a temporary triumvirate to run the state. One of the three selected was Juárez. Within a month, however, another member of the triumvirate, José Simeón Arteaga was named governor and Juárez returned to his less significant position as prosecutor; soon he had the judicial system reorganized and found himself appointed President of the Tribunal of Justice of the state, or essentially chief justice.[21]

It is difficult to realize as these relatively unimportant events were transpiring in Oaxaca that war had already begun between the United States and Mexico. The possibility, if not the probability, of war had existed from the time the United States had annexed Texas in late 1844, but the danger increased after the election to the U.S. presidency of the expansionist James K. Polk and the failure, in fact inability, of the Mexican Government to satisfy Polk's demands for settlement of outstanding debts due American citizens. It was only after General Zachary Taylor moved American troops south of the Nueces River into disputed territory north of the Rio Grande that an actual cause for war was found. In April and May, 1846, clashes occurred between Americans and Mexicans and both nations officially declared war.

At this point one of those almost impossible events in history took place. Santa Anna, in "permanent" exile, convinced Gómez Farías that he had become converted to federalism and wished to serve his country militarily against the invading U.S. forces. He simultaneously convinced Polk that allowing him to return to Mexico would enable him to work out a satisfactory arrangement with the United States. Thus it was that Santa Anna was allowed to pass through a U.S. naval blockade and enter Mexico at Veracruz. On December 6, he was again elected president, *in absentia,* with Gómez Farías again his vice-president. In retrospect Santa Anna's plan is clear. He intended to put the burden and blame for raising funds to fight the war upon Gómez Farías while he took the glory of anticipated military victory.[22]

Among those who appeared in Mexico City on that December 6 to reestablish a revised Constitution of 1824 and take the necessary steps to finance the war was Juárez, one of nine delegates elected from Oaxaca.[23] When Gómez Farías took office as acting president on December 23, he faced a rapidly deteriorating situation. Santa Anna was in San Luis Potosí at the head of the army preparing for the campaign against the invader and the government's most urgent need was funds for this purpose.

On January 11, 1847, the Vice-President decreed the nationalization and sale at public auction of clerical assets valued at
15,000,000 pesos. As time was needed to determine in detail the
value of properties nationalized, the government ordered the
immediate seizure of properties estimated at 10,000,000 pesos
on January 15.[24] Juárez was a member of the committee that
recommended these actions to the executive, but he later commented that the original proposals were amended to the point
that the law became ineffective.

However ineffective Juárez felt the law might be, the pre-
dictable clerical opponents arose. Troops in Mexico City, primarily from upper-class and conservative families, refused to
move toward Veracruz and the Americans and, instead, mutinied
against Gómez Farías, the Congress, and the actions of the government against clerical properties. These *polkos,* as they were
known, caused little bloodshed but stirred up considerable
trouble in the capital. Santa Anna, who had just lost a battle to
Taylor's forces at Buena Vista but had managed to present it
as a victory, took this occasion to return to Mexico City to
restore order. He once again deposed his vice-president, send-
ing him into exile, and on March 29, 1847, announced the
repeal of the anticlerical laws but not before receiving a promise
on the previous day that the church would guarantee a loan of
one and one-half million pesos to enable him to continue the
war.[25] With this, Juárez's career as a national legislator came to
an end. What may well have been his first visit to Mexico City
had produced little to cause the memory of the Oaxacan to be
enhanced. He apparently said little during the debates and
other than his participation in the drafting of the laws regarding church properties is not remembered for any legislative
contribution. By August he had decided to return home and
resume the practice of law and, perhaps, help defend Oaxaca
against the American invasion.

In the state of Oaxaca the *polkos* rebellion had had its supporters and they had managed to seize control of the state government. Knowing this, the delegates to the national congress
had been successful in enacting a law calling for the removal
of this rebel force. Due to the importance of the money and
supplies coming from Oaxaca no serious effort had been made
to enforce this law, however. Juárez, working with liberals in

the state who had consistently opposed the *polkos,* was finally able to have the officials declared unconstitutional and removed. Thus, in October, a temporary government was installed, a legislature convened, and a governor elected. The man elected on a *pro tempore* basis was Benito Juárez. In August of the following year he was elected to a full term as governor of this state. He had come a long way from the village of San Paulo Guelatao, and yet, he was still only forty-one miles away.

Juárez's realization of his closeness to the people comes through clearly in the following sentences from his second inaugural address. He said:

I am a son of the people, and I shall not forget it; on the contrary, I shall uphold their rights, I shall take care that they become educated, that they lift themselves up, that they make a future for themselves, and that they abandon the life of disorder, vice, and misery to which they have been led by men who only with their words proclaim themselves their friends and liberators, but who by their acts show themselves to be the most cruel tyrants.[26]

Certainly, the new governor's actions and attitudes indicate a sincere belief that he could and should work for the benefit of the people from whom he had sprung.

Juárez was never an imposing figure in appearance, being only a little over five feet tall with the dark complexion of his Zapotec origins. He usually dressed in dark clothing and was to be remembered for his modesty rather than flamboyance. He was by nature taciturn and, though he could on occasion inspire by his words, it was because of his sincerity rather than the brilliance of his phrases. He is better remembered for his patience and hard work, even a kind of stubborn doggedness, than for dramatic actions. He was a man who kept much to himself, had few close friends, and was abstemious in his personal habits. In sum, Juárez was not a man whose leadership qualities were immediately apparent. It took time and perhaps the right circumstances for his abilities to make themselves felt and for the people to appreciate what he had to offer them and the nation.

Whether because Juárez was by nature a compromiser or whether he felt more extreme measures would only result in failure, as governor he sought the cooperation of the clergy of

Oaxaca and avoided actions that would alienate the more conservative elements of his state. This meant among other things
that he continued to collect the tithes under existing laws even
though liberals had long argued against compulsory tithes. He
also defended the church's titles to their properties and regularly reiterated his belief in the Catholic Church and its religious
precepts.[27] It would be difficult to argue that Juárez's conciliatory approach brought the end of clerical resistance to liberal ideas, but it is true that the clergy cooperated with the state
in programs of road construction and the building of port facilities on the Pacific coast. As a result over sixty miles of roads
were constructed and a step had been taken toward the unifying
of the state. An effort also was made to remove the internal
obstacles to trade but traditional defense of these customs duties
was too great.[28]

It is doubtful that the clergy looked with equal favor on
Juárez's efforts in the field of education, given their usual fear
of anything that threatened the church's monopoly in that field.
Nevertheless, under Juárez, the state constructed several hundred new schools along with eight new normal schools and serious
efforts were made to provide educational opportunities for
girls, who traditionally had been denied even elementary programs. Juárez did not forget his own Institute of Sciences and
Arts but reorganized it and provided for its support. Equally
educational and perhaps more immediately productive were
programs to introduce new crops and new agricultural practices
to the people of the state in an effort to increase state and individual revenues. A small assist to mining came with the establishment of a mint. Juárez also reorganized the National Guard,
placing it under a competent commander, made arrangements
for better arms and matériel, established a military hospital and
provided pensions for widows of veterans.[29]

Amazingly, though many of Juárez's programs involved significant expenditures, he was able to reduce the debt of the state
and, had it not been for the war with the United States and the
unsettled conditions it produced as well as a cholera epidemic
that hit Oaxaca, he might well have eliminated it altogether.
There were no secrets involved in his approach. He simply did
a good job of collecting existing taxes and reducing unnecessary
expenditures. Luckily, the state of Oaxaca had managed to main-

tain a reasonably thriving economy throughout the difficult times of the nation and this, no doubt, made the financial task easier. It is also probably true that Juárez, by paying civil servants on time and by reducing past practices of favoritism and nepotism, was able to bring a greater degree of honesty and ability into the state offices. Whether or not Juárez succeeded in raising the general level of life in his state as he hoped is difficult to measure with inadequate information and statistics; but the high regard in which he was held by the people of Oaxaca and the lack of substantial criticism of his efforts while governor even by his detractors would suggest that he was at least a capable administrator.[30]

However much Juárez may have wished to avoid it, he could not keep national events from threatening the stability of his administration. In fact, at the time of his first inauguration as governor, there was real danger that the state might be invaded by American forces or that the Mexican nation would disappear as a viable entity.

Under the leadership of Juárez and others the state of Oaxaca consistently provided men and money for the prosecution of the war, in contrast to the reassertion of local autonomy on the part of most of the states. The regionalism with which Gálvez had attempted to cope in the late colonial period and which Santa Anna had ignored with his efforts at centralism in the late 1830s was still very much alive. Oaxaca stood almost alone as a state where liberal, federal-minded leadership could survive and still show concern for the need for national cohesion. The basic contradiction between local economic and political demands and liberal ideology at the national level was yet to be faced. For the moment, however, the leadership of Oaxaca could not be faulted in its dedication to the immediate needs of the nation.[31]

Fortunately, the treaty of Guadalupe Hidalgo ending the war was signed in early 1848 when the Americans located Manuel de la Peña y Peña, who as chief justice became president after the flight from Mexico City of Santa Anna. Actually, fighting continued on a guerrilla basis after the treaty, and the unwelcome American visitors were cause enough for riots or incidents endangering all parties. Santa Anna himself took the lead for a brief period in organizing such guerrilla movements to the south of the national capital but was forced to be constantly on the move to avoid capture. On one such occasion he arrived in Tehuacán on the border of Oaxaca and apparently hoped to move on to Oaxaca. Juárez, seeing the danger to the state from Santanista supporters internally and possible American pursuit from outside, took steps to turn Santa Anna away should he attempt to assume any powers. While Santa Anna paused briefly just inside Oaxaca, he moved on to the east and eventually departed for Jamaica. Though Santa Anna expressed the belief that Juárez was simply getting even with him for the humiliation he had felt when he served the general dinner in those earlier student days, Juárez insisted that his actions were taken only in the interest of the political stability of Oaxaca, and at the request of other state officials.[32]

Partly as a reflection of die-hard conservative feelings and partly as a result of localistic feelings, a rebellion broke out in Tehuantepec in October, 1850, requiring the use of force to end it. Juárez was lenient with the rebels, but at least one leader was executed and another sent into exile.[33] Tragedy struck the state and Juárez on another front earlier in the same year when a major cholera epidemic broke out and killed over ten thousand persons. Though the governor took quick and conscientious efforts in the area of health services, the damage was still great. Early in the epidemic Juárez's two-year-old daughter Guadalupe died. Her death provided still another example of Juárez's abiding belief in living by the law, at least as he saw the law. A municipal cemetery had been established outside the city of Oaxaca some years earlier to prevent unhygienic burials in the church cemetery, but custom had been too strongly established and the law had frequently been ignored. Juárez, though exempt from the law as governor, buried his own daughter in the municipal cemetery and, by example as well as insistence, increased the application of this rather necessary health ordinance.[34]

Whatever the problems of the state of Oaxaca, those of the nation were hardly less serious during the years Juárez served as governor. Following the departure of the American troops and Santa Anna, the temporary government under Peña y Peña had been followed by two moderate liberal presidents, Herrera and Mariano Arista. The election of Herrera was something of a vindication for a man who had fallen partly because of his willingness to negotiate with the United States in the months preceding the war, but the omens were highly unfavorable for his finishing out his term in office.[35] As Hubert H. Bancroft expressed the situation:

Nothing could be more trying than the position of Herrera's government. It was expected to resurrect the country, reorganize departments, aid institutions, and restore prosperity generally; and all this without means, and in the face of violent opposition from parties intent only on their own advancement, and ready to plunge the nation into greater troubles by fomenting outbreaks in different quarters.[36]

In spite of the omens, Herrera survived almost continuous rebellions, a major uprising by Indians in Yucatán, a declining financial situation, and liberal and conservative political opposition. In 1850 he saw his Minister of Defense, Arista, elected president and could retire to private life. In spite of the apparent honesty and sincerity of Arista, he was not as lucky as his predecessor. In June, 1851, an armed rebellion against Arista in Guanajuato favored the return of Santa Anna. A year later, in July, a hatmaker colonel, José María Blancarte, pronounced against the governor of Guadalajara and supporters of Santa Anna seized the occasion to make their own move. Though originally a local affair, this *pronunciamiento* was given wider scope by Blancarte after he was flattered into doing so by the conservatives. Shortly thereafter the Plan of Hospicio called for Santa Anna to replace Arista. Other rebellions followed in Michoacán and elsewhere, finally causing Arista to resign on January 5, 1853, leaving the presidency temporarily in the hands of the chief justice, Juan B. Ceballos.[37]

The military and clerical elements were not satisfied, however, and a military move almost immediately overthrew Ceballos and elected Santa Anna. This was not entirely a result of personal attachments to the man, but represented conservative beliefs that control of the government had to be gained before any safe program could be started. Santa Anna was simply an instrument to be used toward this end. This, for example, was evidently the view of Lucas Alamán, a dedicated conservative statesman, who endorsed the plan and was to serve until his death as a restraining influence on Santa Anna. Others, perhaps, saw Santa Anna as the only national *caudillo* capable of restoring order out of the virtual anarchy into which the country had descended. Whatever the combination of reasons, there were many who rejoiced when the president-elect arrived in Veracruz on April 1, 1853.[38]

With the ascension of power of Santa Anna the liberal administration in Oaxaca, as well as those elsewhere, was doomed. Benito Juárez had ended his term as governor in August, 1852, to be succeeded by an equally dedicated liberal, Ignacio Mejía. The new governor had in turn named him director of the Institute of Sciences and Arts and professor of civil law.[39] The Santanistas removed Mejía and replaced him with General Ignacio Martínez Pinollos who removed Juárez from his posts. Faced with constant insults from conservatives as well as a possible attempt on his life, Juárez made a brief attempt to resume the practice of law. In May, 1853, however, Juárez was arrested and, after being moved from one location to another, was taken into custody by the son of President Santa Anna for transport to the prison at San Juan de Ulúa in the harbor at Veracruz. There he was given his passport, placed on a ship and destined for exile in Europe. Instead, upon arrival in Havana, Juárez was able to reship for New Orleans where he joined other enemies of Santa Anna in what was to be another formative period in the life of the ex-governor of Oaxaca and a time of exceptional decision for the Mexican nation.

The group of refugees who gathered in New Orleans constantly changed in its makeup and diminished in size the longer the Santanista government held on at home. Among the handful who, with Juárez, remained active in their plans to return and overthrow the dictator, were men like Melchor Ocampo, the exiled governor of Michoacán and acknowledged leader of the refugees; José María Mata from Jalapa who later married Ocampo's daughter; Ponciano Arriaga, a well-known liberal from San Luis Potosí, and former president Juan Bautista Ceballos. Of even more importance to Juárez was a young Cuban exile, Pedro Santacilia, who became Juárez's son-in-law, family guardian, and constant correspondent in the years that followed. It is difficult, if not impossible, to reconstruct the feelings of frustration, homesickness, true illness, improvidence, and despair that this group of exiles felt. They spent their time searching for good news from home, corresponding with friends in Mexico and the United States, seeking allies for the ultimate victory over Santa Anna and, all the while, trying to survive with what little funds were obtained from home and earned in the menial and odd jobs available to a Mexican in New Orleans.[40]

There can be little doubt that the personal indignities and deprivations suffered in New Orleans had an effect on Juárez. Yet, the poverty of his background and the stolid nature he had already demonstrated would suggest that he endured his exile somewhat better than others. Probably more important in the development of Juárez's thinking were the close associations he formed. There was of course Santacilia who became one of the few personal confidants that Juárez ever had. Then there was Ocampo. Ocampo was a more dashing figure and a far better educated man than Juárez. As governor of Michoacán, he had distinguished himself as a liberal and had come close to being elected vice president. He had traveled in Europe and possessed a more sophisticated and intellectual mind than his colleague from Oaxaca. In New Orleans and later Ocampo influenced Juárez's developing liberalism by discussion and gifts of books as well as by providing the leadership essential to continuing opposition to Santa Anna.[41] Though he and Juárez would have their differences before his untimely death, Ocampo probably influenced Juárez's later political views as much as any single person.

While the exiles plotted and hoped, the administration of Santa Anna was becoming more and more objectionable to liberals inside Mexico. He had lost no time in grasping the ample powers which many of the conservatives were so anxious to bestow upon the central government and its chief executive. The state legislatures were adjourned and the governors were made directly responsible to the president.[42] The death of Lucas Alamán, the ablest conservative statesman, only forty-three days after the inauguration of Santa Anna, left the dictator without a restraining influence and he turned once again to a desire for plunder and applause. Alamán had been the representative of the conservatives in opposition to the strictly personal military group. His successor was equally as conservative but more easily intimidated by Santa Anna. The government took on more and more the appearance of a monarchy with all the royal trappings. "His Most Serene Highness," as Santa Anna contented himself to be called, became even more corrupt, tyrannical, and vulgar. "Never had the Republic been mired any deeper in the muck of ignorance, want and vice," wrote the Mexican historian, Justo Sierra; "never had the Republic sported such gorgeous plumes."[43]

All of this required money, however, and even Santa Anna, who was unusually successful along this line, was unable to obtain the necessary funds. Thus, as the treasury was depleted, the government began to lose the support of many of its generals and bureaucrats.[44] The revolutionary movement, which was slowly but constantly gaining strength, had its stronghold in the state of Guerrero, where an old liberal, Juan Álvarez, was in control. Álvarez, a veteran of the war for independence, had ruled his department in a semifeudal fashion since the days of Mexico's first president. Since his isolation made him a dangerous enemy, centralist presidents usually recognized him. Santa Anna had made a working agreement with Álvarez, but neither of them was particularly pleased with the situation and, by February, 1854, Guerrero was in virtual open revolt.

On March 1, 1854, a revolutionary plan was proclaimed at the village of Ayutla by an insignificant Colonel Florencio Villareal, withdrawing recognition from the existing government. This Plan of Ayutla was ratified on March 11 with a few amendments at Acapulco by the officers and troops stationed there and by Ignacio Comonfort, a *criollo* recently dismissed from government service by Santa Anna. The adherents of this plan pledged that the army would be sustained, provided for the formation of provisional governments, promised that a constituent congress would be convoked when a majority of the states had accepted the revolution, and invited Álvarez, Tomás Moreno, and Nicolás Bravo to assume leadership of the insurgent forces.[45]

Santa Anna attempted to put down the rising opposition. He was aided by the ten million dollars which he received from the sale of the Mesilla Valley in northern Mexico to the United States. The outcome of the revolutionary movement became more certain during the spring of 1855 when many of the leaders of northern Mexico declared in favor of the Plan of Ayutla and threw their own forces into the struggle against Santa Anna. After two unsuccessful attempts to defeat the rebels in the spring and summer and after the failure of another attempted sale of Mexican territory to the United States, Santa Anna faced the inevitable. When he learned that even his home district of Veracruz had pronounced against him, he made arrangements for his family, and on the morning of August 13, 1855, slipped out of Mexico City to sail four days later into exile, for the third time in his life. The Age of Santa Anna had ended.[46]

The events that transpired in Mexico between the issuance of the Plan of Ayutla and Santa Anna's final defeat were little known and poorly understood by the small group of exiles in the United States. Ocampo had moved to Brownsville in hopes of encouraging revolution in the north, but his success is impossible to measure. Juárez stayed in New Orleans, working in a print shop, rolling cigars, or bordering on starvation but constantly exchanging news with Ocampo and others. There were rumors of the death of Álvarez or of the imprisonment of friends and, on rare occasion, of the defection of some opponent of Santa Anna. Finally, at the end of June, 1855, on the request of Comonfort and with financial aid from Ocampo, Juárez ended his eighteen months of exile when he set sail from New Orleans for Acapulco.[47] During his six weeks at sea the final blows that brought Santa Anna tumbling occurred. Thus, Juárez joined the camp of Álvarez only a few days before the abdication of Santa Anna. Perhaps typically, Juárez made his presence known almost accidentally and began to serve as a political adviser in the revolutionary camp—concerned now with the direction of a program rather than with the man Santa Anna.

There was sufficient cause for concern and for Juárez's urgent call to Ocampo, Mata, and Arriaga to join him in Mexico. In San Luis Potosí a dissident conservative, Antonio Haro y Tamariz, had issued his own plan against Santa Anna and in Guanajuato the moderate Manuel Doblado issued still another. The army of Santa Anna that remained in and around Mexico City came under the control of General Martín Carrera who now proclaimed for the Plan of Ayutla. For a few weeks the country was in confusion, the revolutionists being unable to agree on a single leader.[48] Under the skillful persuasion of Comonfort, however, Haro y Tamariz and Doblado, at a meeting at Lagos de Moreno on September 16, accepted Juan Álvarez as chief of the revolution.[49] Carrera, who had been named interim president by those who hoped to subvert the revolution, resigned and the army put its trust in Comonfort. Álvarez was still the symbol of unity needed by the rebellion he had headed and, uncertain though he was of his ability to lead the nation, he convoked a congress of delegates at Cuernavaca, as promised earlier at Ayutla, to elect a president. Comonfort had supporters and, had he been so inclined, might have been able to seize power and Ocampo also received some votes, but the choice of the congress on October 4, 1855 was still Álvarez for the interim presidency.[50] It remained for a cabinet to be appointed and the new government to begin functioning in the capital.

In spite of disappointed supporters, the major choices for the cabinet were reasonably predicable. Comonfort was named Minister of War and placed in charge of the reorganization and thereby the conserving of the army against those liberals who preferred to rely on state militias. Ocampo had joined the ranks soon enough to obtain two posts for himself, the departments of the Interior and Foreign Relations. A fairly well-known poet, orator, journalist, and frequent bureaucrat, Guillermo Prieto, was named to the Treasury. Juárez, with some apparent reluctance, accepted the post as Minister of Justice and Public Instruction.[51] While Ocampo had something to do with the choices of Juárez and Prieto, it is apparent that those two appointees were seen as strong liberals, or *puros* like Ocampo, as opposed to the moderate, or *moderado,* position of Comonfort. Coincidentally, all the members of Álvarez's cabinet were Masons and most were anticlerical, but division was apparent even before the new government had begun to function, and the weeks ahead demonstrated that conservatism was not the only obstacle to stability in the Mexican government.[52] For Juárez it was again a time of prominence on the national stage, but also a time for difficult and complicated decision.

CHAPTER III

The War of the Reform

THE PROBLEMS OF THE NEW GOVERNMENT WERE MANY. THERE WAS Álvarez himself, an old, inefficient, and rigid republican whose Indian background made him anathema to some and whose crude, disruptive supporters (*pintos*) alienated others. There were the inevitable problems of reconstruction following a rebellion made even worse by the instability marking the years ever since independence. The conservative allies of Santa Anna rallied behind Comonfort, whose moderation and support of military officials still in office offered hope for the future. Ocampo along with Prieto, and perhaps Juárez, wished to push rapidly for far-reaching reforms only to find the way blocked by the uncertain president and the fear of Comonfort that a bloodbath would be unleashed if the program moved too fast.[1] Comonfort even objected to an almost standard tenet of reform thought that excluded members of the clergy from participation in the election of deputies to the congress. Though he lost out on this issue, his opposition was so successful that Ocampo resigned his ministry within a fortnight. Juárez and Prieto considered resigning but were prevailed upon to stay for a while longer.

As the opposition to Álvarez grew and Comonfort leaned more and more to the moderate position, Prieto too resigned. Juárez chose to remain for a few more weeks, in part because he had been preparing what was to become one of the most important of that set of laws known as the Reform Laws. A visitor to Mexico City at about this time described Juárez as a reserved and circumspect man who would not issue any decrees except those that were necessary.[2] Almost exactly one month after this comment the necessary was published as law. The Ley Juárez of November 23 reorganized the judicial system, removing all special tribunals except the military and ecclesiastical, and removing from those all civil jurisdiction.[3]

Though the new law was really quite moderate, it did promise more to come in the future and indicated that the Revolution of Ayutla was not like its predecessors in the history of the nation. There was here the inherent assumption that the grant of equality before the law to all citizens would, in turn, lead to greater equality of opportunity. The new law, however, was considerably misunderstood and interpreted as being a direct attack upon the clergy. Predictably, then, it created a furor. The discontent was brought to a head by a revolutionary movement in Guanajuato, headed by Manuel Doblado, which refused further recognition of Álvarez's government and proclaimed Comonfort president. On December 8, 1855, Álvarez issued a decree appointing Comonfort substitute president during his own temporary absence, and on December 11, publicly surrendered the office to him.[4] In the maneuvering that took place prior to this action, Juárez asked for the acceptance of his resignation of the previous October.[5] Comonfort, upon assuming office, recognized the usefulness of Juárez, however, and though probably happy to have him out of the national government, named him governor of Oaxaca.[6] By the end of the month the Zapotec Indian who had served briefly on the national stage was back within a few miles of his birthplace.[7] But the direction of the movement he had helped to instigate would not allow him to remain there for many months.

The moderates had won, but at least there was a government and it had a program. One of the first acts of Comonfort was the formation of an *estatuto orgánico* in place of a constitution that was in the process of being drafted. This plan, issued on May 15, 1856, provided for centralization in governmental power and, at the same time, placed definite limits on the power of the executive. Provisions were made for a bill of rights, for the prohibition of slavery, for freedom from forced loans, and prohibition of civil and political distinctions based on birth, origin, or race. Ecclesiastics were barred from participation in popular elections and free private instruction was permitted.[8] Even more importantly, the new program promised economic reforms: a new tariff law, funds for internal improvements, revisions in the system of entailed estates, and a law making it easier for foreigners to acquire real estate.[9]

The new government, by attempting to advance a reform

and at the same time be conciliatory, failed to satisfy either extreme radicals or conservatives. Already in January, 1856, a rebellion led by Haro y Tamariz and certain clergymen had raised an army and taken control of the city of Puebla. Although not all of the clergy, including especially Bishop Labastida of Puebla, participated in the revolt, the situation was sufficiently serious to cause Comonfort to lead an army that in March lay siege to the city and forced its surrender by March 22.[10] Because of clerical participation in the revolt, and in spite of his wish to be conciliatory toward the clergy, Comonfort decided to levy an indemnity against the church in Puebla. The controversy that followed even caused him to exile the formerly cooperative bishop and lose further conservative support for his government.[11]

Meanwhile, liberals began to attack the rather highly centralized government that Comonfort had instituted. Though the attack against the *estatuto orgánico* centered in congress, a few of the state governors, including Juárez, refused to enforce it. Some opposed the organic state because they truly believed that a Comonfort dictatorship was planned while others disliked the fact that it deprived them of the unlimited powers which they had been exercising. Luckily, however, a temporary truce was worked out since the existing government was at least preferable to the anarchy which it had brought to an end.[12] As Juárez carefully phrased it, "the government was prudent enough not to insist on compliance."[13]

Actually, radical fears of Comonfort's government should have been assuaged in part by the issuance on June 25, 1856, of one of the most penetrating reform laws the nation had yet enacted. Issued by the Minister of the Treasury, Miguel Lerdo de Tejada, this so-called Ley Lerdo called for the sale by civil and ecclesiastical corporations of all real properties held by them.[14] The law did not confiscate church property since it permitted corporations to make conventional sales of their estates and it was not designed for government revenue, for aside from a five per cent sales tax, the public treasury was to receive nothing. The economic intent of disentailment was to lead to an increase in the purchase and sale of property and thus presumably to economic progress. Socially, the law was designed to produce a group of property owners loyal to the liberal regime.[15]

Although the law did not produce the hoped-for results, still another cause for disaffection by conservatives with the Comonfort government had been introduced.

During this period the congress, in addition to its legislative function, had been drafting a new constitution. After months of argument the constitution was completed on February 5, 1857, and promulgated a week later.[16] In this document the Ayutla revolution was consummated. A federal system of government was constituted with indirect election of the president, the legislature, and the members of the Supreme Court. An unusually full and explicit bill of rights was included and the Ley Juárez and Ley Lerdo were incorporated into the constitution. Although there was no explicit adoption of Catholicism, there was no open statement of religious freedom. Elections were called for the first congress and president under the new constitution and for members of the Supreme Court, the president of which was also to act as vice-president of the republic.

During these months of controversy between the congress and Comonfort and the increasing concern of conservatives about the direction of the government, Juárez was busy with the affairs of Oaxaca. He set about restoring stable government and removing those who had cooperated with Santa Anna. At the same time he attempted to enact measures that would insure competent liberal support in the years ahead. He reorganized and recruited a national guard and persuaded the national government to provide the needed matériel and supplies. He reestablished the Institute and provided classes there in military functions. He relied, at the same time, upon his skill and prestige to settle other state matters. From April until May, 1857, he visited Tehuantepec to attempt to settle a quarrel between that town and Juchitán and to reincorporate the isthmus into the state of Oaxaca from which it had been separated under Santa Anna. This he succeeded in accomplishing to the praise of the Mexico City press.[17]

As previously mentioned, Juárez was one of the state governors who objected to the attempted centralization of power by Comonfort under the temporary government. Fortunately, Comonfort made no serious effort to carry out his plan in Oaxaca and a serious confrontation with Juárez was avoided. When the Ley Lerdo was announced, however, Juárez made his support clear even to the point of purchasing a small piece of property belonging to the church.[18] With the publication of the Constitution of 1857, Juárez took the necessary steps to establish it in Oaxaca. A new state legislature was elected and Juárez was overwhelmingly elected governor. Church officials in the state attempted to embarrass him by closing the doors of the cathedral on the day of his inauguration and thus causing him to use force to open them. Juárez avoided the trap by simply arguing that the religious ceremony was unnecessary since civil officials should be separated from religious matters.

The clerical opposition in Oaxaca was only intensified at the national level. A national decree had been passed requiring all public officials to take an oath of obedience to the constitution. The Archbishop replied by ordering the clergy not to take the oath and gave instructions on how to deal with those persons who did take the oath. Such persons could not receive an ecclesiastical burial nor could masses be said for those who died without a retraction. In addition, priests could not hear confessions from those who had taken the oath. These same restrictions applied to anyone who had taken over church property under the provisions of the Ley Lerdo.[19] Further fuel was added to the already flaming clerical fears when another reform law was enacted on April 11, 1857, secularizing the cemeteries and regulating the amount and collection of fees charged by the clergy for their services.[20]

Despite the virtually impossible conditions under which Comonfort labored, with opposition to the new constitution coming from all sides and his own personal reservations about it, presidential elections were held under its terms. For a brief time radicals sought the candidacy of Miguel Lerdo de Tejada as an opponent to Comonfort, but after his withdrawal the constitutional election of Comonfort was automatic.[21] In spite of his withdrawal, Lerdo received some votes in the rather confusing national election and Juárez also received a handful. More importantly, Juárez was elected president of the Supreme Court in the same election, thus becoming next in line for the presidency.[22]

The inauguration of a new government did not quiet the apprehensions across the nation.[23] Comonfort wavered in the face of continual attacks and evidently hoped that some compromise could still be reached. Feeling the need for stronger power than the new constitution granted him, he asked for a suspension of the guarantees of civil liberty and a virtual revision of the entire constitution. Congress at first refused, waiting to see the makeup of the new cabinet. The appointments, especially that of Juárez as Secretary of *Gobernación*, seem to have satisfied congress because shortly thereafter the enlarged presidential powers were granted. Whatever Comonfort's motives may have been in appointing Juárez, the Oaxacan was explicit in his acceptance. Writing to the undersecretary of government, Juárez avowed that it was every citizen's duty to do whatever he could in support of the nation at such a critical time and his own convictions placed him in the position of cooperating in every way "in the development of the glorious revolution of Ayutla."[24]

In spite of the government's increased power, however, small revolts continued across the country and by November there were rumors of an impending major revolt. The military and clerical groups took advantage of Comonfort's desire for a stronger executive as a point of attack and, on December 17, 1857, Félix Zuloaga, the general in command at Tacubaya, declared in favor of a Comonfort dictatorship and another constitutional convention.[25] Comonfort hesitated while Zuloaga took possession of the capital, dissolved congress, and arrested Juárez and others. On December 19, still hoping that he could hold extremists on both sides in check, Comonfort accepted the Plan of Tacubaya and declared a state of siege, asserting that the military authority had assumed all the power in order to re-establish public order.

While Juárez was imprisoned in the palace for three weeks, Comonfort foolishly awaited announcements of support for his stand from liberal leaders throughout the nation. The conservatives became even more suspicious of him and in January another pronouncement was issued by Zuloaga removing Comonfort from the presidency. Realizing that civil war could no longer be averted, Comonfort again reversed his position, released Juárez and raised an army to recover control of the capital. The effort was futile, however, and on January 21, 1858, Comonfort left Mexico on his way to exile in the United States. The following day Zuloaga was declared president by a *junta* in Mexico City and conservative armies were gathered to eliminate the liberals.[26]

A number of liberals, including the governors of several states, had already declared that Comonfort had broken his oath to the constitution and forfeited the presidency, thus making Juárez the constitutional president of Mexico. Juárez, himself, after arriving in Guanajuato following his release from confinement, issued a proclamation to the nation on January 19, announcing his assumption of the executive power and plans to form a government.[27]

Thus was the stage set for a three-year period of civil strife known as the War of the Reform. This was only part of the long struggle to destroy the power and political influence of the privileged classes in Mexico. Their power and influence, which had been inherited from Spanish colonial times, was enjoyed especially by the church, which had become wealthy through centuries of prestige and social domination, and by the army, virtually an upper-class closed corporation, with its closely guarded traditions and its aristocratic character. This was, then, a struggle of the ecclesiastical and certain military elements to maintain their social and political supremacy, now threatened by the new constitutional provision for social equality, free thought and speech, and by its provisions against *fueros,* ecclesiastical properties, and participation by the clergy in politics.[28] By the spring of 1858 the lines of battle were fairly well drawn with most of the capital and federal district and the states of Puebla and Tlaxcala and parts of San Luis Potosí in the pro-Tacubaya camp surrounded by a constitutionalist coalition made up of Querétaro, Guanajuato, Aguascalientes, Zacatecas, Jalisco, Colima, Michoacán, Veracruz, and Guerrero. In general, it evolved into a war of the states around the periphery of the country against those in the center.[29] The potential outcome was very much in doubt.

Shortly after Juárez's arrival in Guanajuato, a local resident wrote to a friend in Mexico City, "An Indian by the name of Juárez, who calls himself President of the Republic, has arrived in this city."[30] To be sure, Juárez, in spite of his past public posts, was not yet a hero of the nation and his pretension to the presidency was at least debatable. Fortunately, he had the support of important local leaders like Doblado in Guana-juato, Santos Degollado in Michoacán, and Arteaga in Colima. In addition, he named to his cabinet his fellow refugee in the United States, the capable and inspiring Ocampo, as Minister of War; a former fellow student and proven liberal, Manuel Ruíz, as Minister of Justice; the increasingly important and helpful Prieto as Minister of the Treasury and the younger and less-well-known León Guzman as Minister of *Fomento*. The command of the army of the coalition of states supporting the Juárez government was given to General Anastasio Parrodi. In the first flush of conflict Parrodi convinced the constitutionalist leaders that victory could be won quickly if the enemy could be drawn away from its home base in pursuit of Juárez. With this in mind, Juárez and his government moved to Guadalajara where they arrived by mid-February and let loose a rash of cor-respondence to raise men and money in support of the liberal armies. The plan almost proved fatal.

Zuloaga had at the outset the abler generals, including him-self, Miguel Miramón, Luis G. Osollos, Tomás Mejía, and Leonardo Márquez, as well as the better disciplined armies. In addition, the conservatives could depend upon the assistance of the clergy, which had the wealth to contribute to the financing of the civil war in spite of the loss of a great deal of property as a result of the Ley Lerdo. In anticipation of this, Zuloaga had taken immediate steps to restore the privileges of the church and to obtain large sums of money from church leaders to finance the government as well as the armies.[31] Thus it was that Miramón, Mejía, and Zuloaga were well equipped to march north in answer to Parrodi's challenge. The result was almost the exact opposite of liberal hopes. Osollos decisively defeated a liberal coalition under Parrodi at Salamanca, Guanajuato, on March 9–10, after a display of superior generalship on the part of the conservatives and unpardonable errors by the liberals. This first major battle of the war caused consternation in the liberal camp as it opened the gates to the interior to their foes. It was followed two days later by the capitulation of Manuel Doblado at Silao and his promise to withdraw from the fighting in return for his personal freedom. Parrodi retreated with the remnants of an army to Guadalajara where he was joined by Degollado.

Clearly it was going to take time for the raw undisciplined

militia of the states loyal to Juárez to develop into armies. It was going to require greater tenacity than had been foreseen on the part of the nonprofessional military men who led the liberal armies to protect and preserve the republican movement.[32]

The liberal government almost came to a dramatic end off the battlefield only a few days after the defeat at Salamanca. In Guadalajara, on the morning of March 13, a group of soldiers rebelled within the palace and imprisoned Juárez and his cabinet. While armistice discussions were underway, another group of loyal troops attacked from outside, convincing the rebels that they should immediately execute the president. Prieto's loyalty and eloquence paid off, however, because he jumped in front of Juárez and persuaded the soldiers to put down their guns and then to release him.[33] Following this near tragedy, the liberals prepared to remove their government to Veracruz, anticipating an attack on Guadalajara by the conservatives. Since it was considered too dangerous to attempt to cross the nation, the decision was made to move to the west coast and board ship for the safer city of Veracruz.

In spite of the precautions that were taken to move the "sick family," as the Juárez government was now being called, the conservatives almost captured Juárez while he was en route to Colima. The *juaristas* successfully fought off the attackers, however, only to arrive on March 25 to learn that the conservatives had seized Guadalajara and Parrodi had surrendered. Juárez named Degollado to replace Parrodi as Minister of War and Commander of the Army of the North and West and continued with his preparations for the trip to Veracruz. On April 8, Juárez and his party crossed to the small fishing village of Manzanillo where they took a ship three days later for Acapulco and Panama.[34] At Panama they crossed by railroad to Colón where they boarded a steamer bound for New Orleans by way of Havana. Finally, after a few days revisiting scenes of their former exile, Juárez and his official family embarked for Veracruz where they arrived on May 4 to the welcome of Governor Manuel Gutiérrez Zamora.[35] Though a reasonably safe location for the liberal government had been found, there was little else to cheer the arriving Juárez. The conservatives had been winning victories throughout the early months of 1858 and continued to do so. San Luis Potosí was occupied and Vidaurri, who had been moving down from the north, was defeated and driven back into Nuevo León. After the fall of Guadalajara most of the Pacific coast had fallen under conservative control. About the only bright spot in the military picture during 1858 was the fact that, even though the conservatives controlled most of the towns, the guerrilla bands of liberals often held the countryside and constantly threatened that control. Still, a few really important liberal victories were needed before the conservative confidence in ultimate victory could be seriously shaken.

In spite of the strength of the conservative position, dissension was developing within the Zuloaga administration. The conservative president had fought with the liberals during the Revolution of Ayutla and had never gained the complete confidence of the clergy. In addition, the conservative party had split into factions over the advisability of retaining Zuloaga as president. The temporary constitution under which he governed pleased no one and it also failed to establish any regularity or order in governmental practices, since the peculiar circumstances of the conservatives at times compelled them to operate outside the law. The seriousness of the situation became evident in the last week of December when some of the troops of the capital turned against Zuloaga in a coup d'etat which overthrew him temporarily and was thwarted only by the return of Miramón and his army. The respite was only a brief one, however, for by the end of January Zuloaga relinquished the presidency in favor of Miramón.³⁶

The first aim of the new conservative president was the capture of Veracruz. Miramón took charge of the campaign, but he failed to take into account the almost impregnable position of the city and the yellow fever which attacked those unaccustomed to the climate of the coast. As a result, the attempted capture of the city in February and March failed completely.³⁷ Still another reason for Miramón's retreat was the fact that Degollado had gathered together a large coalition of troops in Querétaro and Guanajuato and was moving south in the direction of Mexico City. While the liberal army advanced, a conservative force under Márquez and his lieutenant, Mejía, set out from Veracruz to meet it. The liberals actually occupied the outskirts of Mexico City and the capital was declared in a state of siege. Márquez succeeded in entering the city, however, and on

April 10 and 11 attacked Degollado at Tacubaya and administered a decisive defeat. As an aftermath of this defeat the captured liberal officers were shot along with a number of medical students who had gone out from the capital to care for the wounded of both sides. This was not the first instance of the shooting of captive officers during the fighting, but it was the most flagrant example and, among the medical students, involved some of the more prominent Mexican families. Henceforth the war was carried on with even greater animosity than ever before.[38]

While the confusing, but basically unhappy, military scene unfolded, Juárez had been involved in the equally confusing problems of establishing, maintaining, and directing a civil government. There was the constant problem of raising money, spending it wisely and distributing it among the many small military groups supporting the republican cause. There was the further problem of regional rivalries that could be used for or against Juárez. The conservatives of Guadalajara were especially successful in using local self-consciousness to maintain opposition to the republican government. Juárez, however, skillfully took into account federalist demands and the economic needs of the interior or northern provinces to obtain considerable support for his cause. It is no coincidence that much of the area supporting Juárez had long-standing feelings of mistreatment by the central plateau and had frequently expressed the wish for greater local autonomy and economic opportunity.

There was the related problem of obtaining foreign recognition. Most governments had simply recognized Zuloaga after his assumption of the presidency and Juárez saw the extreme importance of at least winning the support of the United States, support that could conceivably take military as well as monetary and diplomatic form. All the while, Juárez must prove himself strong enough to hold together a varied assortment of military and civilian associates, some of them strong-willed, some of them with tendencies to waver in the face of defeat, and most of them with unpredictable temperaments and ambitions.

Degollado, the "Hero of Defeats" as he had become known, had been unusually successful in raising a new army after each defeat, but his desire to avoid further bloodshed might well overcome his dedication to the constitutionalist cause. In fact,

in November, 1859, during a new campaign aimed at the
seizure of Mexico City, he arranged for a meeting with Miramón
near Querétaro to discuss a possible settlement. The move failed
because Miramón refused to accept the command offered if it
meant acceptance of the Constitution of 1857. The following
day, November 13, Miramón decisively defeated Degollado and
Doblado at La Estancia de las Vacas, inflicting extremely heavy
losses on the liberals.[39]

While Degollado wavered, Vidaurri in Nuevo León quit. Concerned with protecting himself against Juárez's control, Vidaurri
had consistently refused to accept orders from the central government. Degollado and other military leaders had finally been
forced to denounce him and, because of their unity, had forced
the resignation and departure from the country of a potentially
valuable ally.[40] Not as significant, perhaps, was the lack of support given to Juárez by Juan Álvarez, still in charge of his personal fief in the state of Guerrero. Oaxaca should have been
solidly in the Juárez camp, but unfortunately for Juárez the
efforts and abilities of Porfirio Díaz were insufficient to prevent
such division in liberal ranks as to allow periodic conservative
control. Doblado, in accordance with his promise and possibly
because of his lack of faith in the victory of Juárez, was still
sitting out the war.

Luckily for Juárez there were a few new leaders emerging
out of the exigencies of the war. Ignacio Zaragoza, an extremely
capable military leader, was actively engaged in the fighting;
Leandro Valle, a young and relatively unknown figure of the
Reform, was emerging as a true leader and Jesús González Ortega, heir to the liberalism of Gómez Farías in Zacatecas, was
beginning to attract attention with his military contributions
as well as his flair for attention. Unfortunately it would take a
while for the new leaders to make their major contributions and
for the problems with the better known older ones to be resolved.

Aside from matters relating to purely military affairs and the
basic issue of survival, Juárez had the responsibility of convert-
ing the Reform into something more than the few laws that had
been issued before the defection of Comonfort. All of the liberal leaders were in general agreement as to their ultimate goals
of stability in government and freedom for the people, but there
was room for much disagreement as to specific steps to be taken

and, especially, the timing of such steps. Even before Juárez had left Guadalajara, various specific proposals had been discussed and the debate had continued in Veracruz. Essentially, Juárez wished to make clear to the people of Mexico his plans and expectations but without increasing the size and vehemence of the opposition.[41] Men like Miguel Lerdo de Tejada and Degollado argued with equal reason, however, that the violence of conservative opposition could hardly be increased whatever might be done. There was also the problem of raising funds to support the republic. The revenues of the port at Veracruz had enabled the government to survive but the conservatives were dipping even more deeply into church funds—a fact that deprived the Juárez government at the time of resources and would in the long run seriously hamper those programs of the republic that cost money.

Finally, after an especially important conference with Degollado, who had traveled all the way from Colima to make his wishes known, Juárez gave in to the pressures from his ministers.[42] Lerdo, no doubt delighted with the decision, brought forth notes from previous cabinet discussions and, after another lengthy discussion with the other ministers, drafted a manifesto to be issued by the government. This statement of July 7 from the constitutional government to the nation, signed by Juárez, Ocampo, Ruíz, and Lerdo, spelled out in broad terms the situation at the moment and the hopes and plans of the government for the future.[43]

The government made clear that immediate laws would be enacted, bringing the clergy under civil control and protecting religious liberty as a prerequisite to economic growth. Though this promise was to become the best remembered and most violently received part of the program, it was only the beginning of a comprehensive plan for the development of Mexico. Judicial reforms were promised, and a massive increase and improvement in education was outlined. Commerce was to be improved by providing greater security on the highways and various obstacles to internal trade were to be removed. The government further believed that vast changes in the field of public finance were needed, including changes in the tax laws, revisions of the commercial regulations then in existence, and a redistribution of the revenues available to the states and to the federal government.

The government intended to reduce the public debt, partly by requiring that government bonds be used as part of the purchase price of church properties soon to be nationalized and the purchase of public lands as well. Other changes in land policy were designed to encourage increased immigration as were plans for the creation of public works projects to create jobs for the new arrivals. New laws were to be passed encouraging investment of private capital in transportation facilities, both roads and railroads.

In spite of the obvious importance of the overall program announced in this manifesto, its significance was overlooked once the specific laws affecting the church were issued. These laws, known generally as the Reform Laws of 1859, produced more immediate results than the more ambitious total program and bolstered the assumptions dating back to the Lerdo law that the church was the prime target of the *juaristas*. Certainly the laws concerning church properties were interpreted as attacks on the God-given right to own property.[44]

The federal government on July 12, 1859, issued the first and most important of the series of new and more drastic decrees against the clergy, and its regulations were published the following day.[45] This declared the nationalization, without compensation, of all church capital and real property. Most importantly to Juárez, the law decreed the separation of church and state and promised equal protection to all religions in the future.[46] All monasteries of the regular orders were suppressed and new ones were prohibited. The buildings were confiscated and the monks were to join the secular clergy while being forbidden to wear their habit or live as a brotherhood. Their churches, other than those designated by the civil authorities as houses of worship, would be sold, together with the monastery buildings. The buildings were to be subdivided and each section appraised separately. This was necessary since few persons could afford to purchase an entire monastery, and the land beneath any subdivision was frequently very valuable. The sections were to be sold at public auction at a price no less than two-thirds of the evaluation. Of this price, at least one-half must be paid in cash and the other half in securities of the national debt. Other details of the regulation spelled out the procedure and terms of payment of mortgages of properties previously or subsequently disentailed under the Ley Lerdo.

For some reason nunneries were treated differently from the monasteries under the law of July 12. They would be allowed to continue, although nuns would have the right to leave the convent and receive financial support in the amount of the dowry they had paid upon entering. No novices were to be admitted in the future.

Other reform laws followed in 1859, making the cemeteries state property, making marriage a civil contract, and providing for legal separation. Still others provided for civil registration of births and deaths, recalling the Mexican legation at the Vatican, and spelling out the rules regarding religious toleration.[47]

In spite of the apparent surprise expressed at the expropriation law by the clergy and their violent response, Juárez had actually only confirmed by his decree policies already being practiced by liberal governors and some generals in the constitutionalist camp. As early as August, 1858, Pedro Ogazón, governor of Jalisco, issued a decree ordering that certain payments on church mortgages be made to the liberal government.[48] Later in December, Degollado issued even harsher decrees ordering disentailment of properties in Guadalajara.[49] These decrees of Degollado coupled with others issued in January from Morelia anticipated by six months much of what the laws from Veracruz in July, 1859, attempted.[50] In Zacatecas, Ortega had also taken actions against clerical properties without consulting Veracruz.[51]

In spite of the financial gains for the constitutionalist government that resulted at times from these new reform laws, there was no great overall improvement in the government's financial position. In fact, Juárez saw the real significance of the new laws in the "absolute independence of the civil power, and religious liberty" that would be achieved with victory.[52] Clearly other means would have to be found to gain the resources needed. Lerdo, who had worked so diligently to bring about the issuance of the new laws, left immediately for the United States, hoping to use clerical lands as a guarantee for loans to Mexico from sources in the United States. Unfortunately for his plans, the Buchanan administration believed success would jeopardize other American interests and his mission failed.[53]

The international complications that interfered with Lerdo were not unique. Both liberals and conservatives had become increasingly concerned with efforts to raise money abroad, considered now the *sine qua non* of victory. The Mexican historian Justo Sierra even believes that "the instinct for self-preservation had come to obliterate every other idea. . . . Both sides allowed themselves to be carried away by this animal instinct and both succumbed to this dissolution of principle."[54] Whether so strong an indictment of both governments is warranted is irrelevant. The fact is that conservatives and liberals alike engaged in negotiations and entered into agreements that are subject to question as to their necessity and value.

As early as February, 1859, John Forsyth, U.S. Minister to the Zuloaga government, discussed with Mexican leaders the possibility of the purchase of transit rights across Tehuantepec and territorial changes in northern Mexico; he reported favorable responses.[55] He might well have succeeded in these discussions since the church was anxious to relieve the financial pressures on the government that made it the victim of frequent requests for funds and occasionally of virtually forced loans. However, a quite undiplomatic exchange between Forsyth and the Mexican Minister for Foreign Affairs, Luis G. Cuevas, over a tax on Americans resident in Mexico, caused Forsyth to break off relations and return home.[56]

Following this fiasco the Zuloaga government, in November, 1859, signed the highly unfavorable Mon-Almonte Treaty with Spain. Mexico received nothing other than the improvement of relations with Spain in return for recognizing both new and previously canceled claims of Spanish citizens against Mexico. The consequences of this agreement were not to be felt until after the military conflict had ended, but the damage was there. A month earlier, Miramón concluded still another foreign financial agreement of little immediate advantage and with unforseen future consequences. In return for somewhat less than one million pesos the Mexican treasury agreed to pay the Swiss banking house of Jecker fifteen million pesos, a debt that was not only unrealistic at the time but a pretext for later direct French involvement in Mexican affairs.[57]

As pointed out, however, the liberals could ill afford to be very critical of these conservative actions since they also fell into the trap of expediency in negotiating with the United States. The Juárez government naturally desired recognition from the United States plus whatever additional aid they might conceivably obtain. Toward this end, Ocampo's son-in-law, José María Mata, was dispatched to Washington as the representative of the Juárez government. Mata quickly reported the almost too obvious desire of Buchanan to obtain transit rights in Tehuantepec plus other territorial concessions by Mexico. He expressed his own belief that some concessions would be advantageous and apparently Juárez was inclined to agree. At least William M. Churchwell, Buchanan's special representative to Mexico, reported this to be the case after a quick tour of Mexico.[58] To act upon these apparently favorable auspices, Buchanan sent Robert M. McLane to Mexico as Minister with authority to recognize the Juárez government if he judged it appropriate. Although McLane found Foreign Minister Ocampo less responsive to an agreement than earlier because of improved military circumstances, he decided to extend recognition on April 7 and prolonged negotiations began.[59]

During the summer various stratagems were tried by both McLane and Ocampo. Particularly important to Ocampo was the protection of Mexico's sovereignty and a virtual defensive alliance with the United States that would bring military assistance upon request. More important to McLane were the various transit routes and the acquisition of Lower California without involving the United States in such direct commitments. By July Ocampo made clear his willingness to negotiate the right of transit across Tehuantepec, with ports of deposit at both ends, as well as transit rights across northern Mexico. He was not, however, willing to consider the cession of Lower California.[60] By August McLane became convinced that the cession of territory was out of the question and continued to press for all other U.S. goals.[61]

The failure of Lerdo's efforts to obtain a loan secured by clerical properties coupled with serious military reverses, including Degollado's defeat at La Estancia, apparently sapped Juárez's ministers of whatever bargaining abilities they had. In any event, on December 14, 1859, Ocampo signed a treaty conceding everything the U.S. had sought except Lower California. Under the terms of the treaty, the United States obtained the Tehuantepec transit as well as rights of way from Texas to the Gulf of California. Especially demeaning were provisions allowing the U.S. to use military forces within these areas almost at will. The United States in return agreed to pay four million dollars, with two of the four millions to be applied to payment of claims of American citizens against the Mexican government.[62]

Reactions to the treaty were unfavorable from almost all quarters. Conservatives naturally opposed any action that might be beneficial to the liberals, but in addition many Mexican liberals felt the clearly implied threat to Mexican sovereignty. Fortunately, perhaps, for Mexico, there was equal and decisive opposition in the United States. Partly out of fear of the expansion of slave-state influence and partly because of a fear of unnecessary involvement in Mexican affairs for the United States, enough members of the U.S. Senate opposed the treaty to effect its defeat.

Efforts by defenders of the treaty in both countries continued until October when the deadline for ratification expired. By that time, however, Juárez, either because Miramón's second siege of Veracruz had just failed or because he had come to have more serious doubts about U.S. intentions, decided against extension of the deadline.[63] Thus ended one of the most debated actions of the long years of the War of the Reform.[64]

Certainly, whatever the course of diplomatic affairs, military events had turned toward the liberals by the middle of 1860. In February, Miramón had launched his second attempt to capture the city of Veracruz. This second siege began exactly one year after the first, lasted the same length of time, and fared no better. The major difference was that this time Miramón attempted to complete the siege by sea. Two small ships, purchased from the Spanish in Cuba, sailed into the harbor to cooperate in the attack. Their appearance, however, had been anticipated by the Juárez government and Juárez issued a proclamation declaring them pirates. Under international law American authorities were asked to pursue the ships and arrest those on board. As a result an American ship in the vicinity captured the transports and took their crews to New Orleans. Regardless of the legality of this American intervention, and an

American judge did order the release of the ships and crews, whatever threat had existed from the sea to Veracruz was removed and at the end of March Miramón raised the siege and returned to his capital to prepare another campaign in the interior.[65] Meanwhile, activities in the interior had increased and in general had been advantageous to the liberals.[66]

Military improvements came slowly, however, and there was a period during the spring and summer when it appeared that neither side was capable of winning. Men as competent and loyal as Degollado and M. Lerdo were increasingly attracted by peace proposals pushed by the British in Mexico. G. B. Mathew, British Minister, even while the second siege of Veracruz was going on, had suggested an armistice of six months to one year during which a new constituent assembly was to be elected. The proposal had enough merit for Juárez's cabinet to debate the subject heatedly on March 13, and commissioners from the opposing governments actually met the following day. Juárez's refusal to sacrifice the Constitution of 1857, as Lerdo and others wished, meant that no agreement with Miramón was possible and the discussions were terminated.[67] Lerdo continued to argue for negotiated settlement within the cabinet, and Degollado, who had been serving briefly as Minister of War, returned to the field with serious doubts as to the correctness of Juárez's decision. Lerdo finally broke completely with Juárez over a proposal to suspend payments on the foreign debts as a temporary means to avoid complete bankruptcy. Though Juárez accepted this proposal on May 29, he reversed his position the following day and Lerdo felt he had no choice but to leave the cabinet.[68]

Indications of dissension in liberal ranks continued to plague Juárez in spite of growing evidence of liberal military superiority. Some of this dissension was based upon a sincere conviction but clearly some was the result of conflicting personal ambitions. The results were equally disturbing, whatever the cause. In March and April Vidaurri made a definite move in Nuevo León to set up a separate government to be composed, at least at first, of the states of Zacatecas and Nuevo León.[69] Doblado, who favored a moderate liberal scheme to arrange for the return of Comonfort, seems to have considered Vidaurri's plan for a time although he had little in common with Vidaurri outside of a personal desire for power. Doblado denied any such thoughts, but the rumors were numerous.[70] Though nothing very specific came of any of these plans, evidence of criticism to and about Juárez continued to appear.

Luckily for the political stability Juárez sought, the liberal armies began to win truly significant military victories. On June 15, 1860, Ortega, who had just been named military commander of liberal forces in four states, defeated a conservative army at Peñuelas, Aguascalientes, in what was to become one of the most significant battles of the war.[71] Following Peñuelas, Ortega consolidated his forces at Lagos, Jalisco, where he was joined by Zaragoza, Doblado, Berriozábal, and other liberal leaders. On August 10, this coalition marched against Miramón in the Silao hills of Guanajuato and completely routed him. Silao, Querétaro, Celaya, and Guanajuato were occupied while Miramón fled to Mexico City.[72]

The conservatives found it difficult to believe that defeat was so near. The entire republic, except the cities of Guadalajara, Tepic, Mexico, and Puebla, was now under liberal control as a result of their recent successes.[73] Even when news reached Mexico City that Ortega was planning to move in that direction, there were many persons who refused to believe it.[74] However, the high command of the conservatives fully recognized the danger of their position.

Ortega's plan to attack Mexico City, however, was delayed by a change in the plans of the liberal leaders. The military contingent from Tamaulipas was called away, reducing the number of forces available, and the weather in the Valley of Mexico rendered military operations virtually impossible. There was in addition a strong conservative force at Guadalajara which Degollado thought should be destroyed before the march on the capital was made. New plans were laid with this objective in mind.[75]

With the sudden massing of large liberal forces in the neighborhood of Mexico City, the financial problem of the liberals became grave. Ortega went to Guanajuato seeking resources, but they were so scarce that another solution had to be found. As early as August 29, Degollado had suggested to Ortega the possibility of seizing a *conducta* (train) carrying silver from the mines in the interior to the coast. The proposal was complicated by the fact that the silver in question was the property of British subjects who would object even to the temporary "borrowing" of their wealth.[76] Doblado acted first, however, and independently. On September 9, Ignacio Echagaray, under orders from Doblado, seized the *conducta* bound for Tampico at Laguna Seca, near San Luis Potosí. On learning of the action, Degollado assumed full responsibility.[77]

Juárez, in spite of the obvious need for money, was appalled at Degollado's decision and ordered that those responsible be reprimanded and the money returned.[78] Whether Juárez acted out of moral conviction or a realistic assessment of the danger of English intervention on the Gulf coast can never be known, but it is true that the liberal armies had studiously avoided interfering with properties belonging to the British whatever their attraction or the liberal needs. As a matter of fact, Juárez need not have reprimanded Degollado; he did enough of that to himself. With the siege of Guadalajara under way and the liberals on the verge of complete victory, Degollado began to have second thoughts and agonized over his decision to allow the silver to be taken. In part he suffered pangs of conscience and in part he may have believed he had threatened the Juárez government with foreign intervention. He also was still under pressure from the British Minister to support means of bringing the war to as rapid a conclusion as possible. In any event, Degollado proposed the immediate return of $400,000 of the *conducta* and proposed a plan of pacification with Mathew as the mediator.[79]

Degollado wrote to Mathew that he did not believe the country could be pacified by the force of arms alone, but only by mutual concessions, and that, although he favored the victory of the liberal principles, he would be willing to compromise in the matter of the form of the institutions and the personnel of the government. He added that if his proposition were rejected by both parties he would retire from public affairs, but if rejected by the conservatives only, he would favor continuing the war. His plan called for a new congress to meet within three months to decree a new constitution on the basis of the reform laws and for members of the diplomatic corps together with representatives of the two rival parties to name a president. The person selected was to be neither Miramón nor Juárez.[80]

Degollado wrote to Juárez informing him of the action he had taken and asserting that Ortega was in accord with the plan and that Doblado would accept any decision of the government. He repeated his promise to resign if Juárez failed to accept his proposal.[81] A meeting of liberal chiefs was called by Ortega to consider the proposal but, on September 30, they unanimously and vehemently rejected it.[82] On October 4, Juárez notified Degollado and Ortega of his rejection of the plan. He pointed out that the war was being fought not over the personality of the president but over questions of fundamental law. To accept Degollado's proposal would, he felt, involve the surrender of all the gains that had been made in three years of fighting and would simply turn Mexico's affairs over to representatives of nations that had supported the conservatives.[83]

The government, already embarrassed by the seizure of the *conducta*, immediately removed Degollado from the command which he only nominally held and ordered him to come to Veracruz. Ortega was named as the new Commander in Chief.[84] Though Ortega's appointment was probably no surprise since he had emerged as the most exciting and most successful military leader of the liberals in the last stages of the war, there was irony in his appointment because he had been involved earlier in a transaction not unlike that of Degollado.

As early as September 18, Ortega had expressed an intention to try to bribe Severo Castillo, the commander of the conservative forces at Guadalajara, and if this failed to try to reach some peaceful agreement for the surrender of the town.[85] Ortega subsequently arranged a meeting with Castillo at which the latter proposed that the Constitution of 1857 be revised and Juárez resign. Ortega agreed that Juárez would resign if he felt the reform program could be advanced and that the reform of the constitution could be done within existing laws.[86] These concessions by Ortega evidently surprised Castillo, who then hedged on his demands with the complaint that someone just as bad as Juárez would become president. The result was a breakdown in the discussions and the necessity to take Guadalajara by force.

Many observers both at the time and later considered Ortega's actions as bad as those of Degollado's in proposing his plan of pacification.[87] Interestingly enough, the only official reprimand that Ortega received was from Degollado, who accused Ortega of

going beyond his legal powers.[88] Juárez not only did not criti-
cize him but shortly thereafter promoted him to the position
formerly held by Degollado. In strict equity, Ortega was as
guilty of disloyalty to the government as his former chief, but
Juárez undoubtedly recognized the value of Ortega's leadership and military ability at such a crucial moment in the conflict.

Juárez's confidence was well placed because, following the
surrender of Guadalajara in late October, Ortega appeared in
the Valley of Mexico at the head of an army of 16,000 men
while Miramón marched out from the city with only 8,000. On
the morning of December 22, Miramón launched a futile attack
on the liberals who occupied the hills around San Miguel Cal-
pulalpan. Within two hours the conservatives were completely
routed and Miramón with other conservative leaders fled back to
the city of Mexico.[89] Miramón considered facing a siege, but
Ortega's insistence on unconditional surrender dissuaded him.
Thus on Christmas Day, 1860, Ortega entered Mexico City at
the head of the first section of his army after Miramón had departed on the previous day.[90] The War of the Reform was over
but the issues over which Mexicans had been dying were far
from settled. The problems of leadership in peace that Juárez
now faced were equal in difficulty to anything he had faced during the previous three years.

CHAPTER IV

Presidency and Intervention

JUÁREZ LEARNED OF ORTEGA'S VICTORY WHILE ATTENDING AN OPERA in Veracruz. Stopping the performance, he quietly informed the audience of the momentous occasion and a night of celebration for the local populace was underway, begun oddly enough when the opera singers burst into a rendition of *La Marseillaise*. The problems of travel would provide Juárez with over two weeks of respite from the responsibilities in Mexico City but he immediately began discussions in person and by correspondence with those leaders of the liberal cause who would make up the government.

There was adequate cause for serious discussion. The problems facing the government were literally innumerable. First and foremost was the problem of finances. This had been a crucial issue during the fighting but would continue to be the most important and impossible issue with which Juárez's ministers would be forced to deal. There were the further complications with foreign nations—the need to settle not only financial questions but diplomatic, personal, and influence questions. The defeat of Miramón had not eliminated all internal military opposition. Márquez and Zuloaga had escaped to the interior along with other less important conservative leaders and military actions would still be needed. Even Miramón who had found refuge aboard a French warship at Veracruz and left the country, could exert influence on Mexican affairs. Aside from forces external to the constitutionalist cause—foreign demands and conservative opponents—there were still horrendous obstacles to an easy transition to peace. The press and related political clubs represented various shades of liberal political opinion as well as the personal political ambitions of the more important liberal figures. It was impossible to please all. There were constitutional questions that the government had never had occasion to face, questions as to the actual powers of the president and the degree of parliamentary control intended. The governors and local leaders had been forced to act independently of the national government during the fighting and, even if they were not reluctant to give up their powers, which they usually were, the precise power relationships would take time to establish. Finally, the very human attitudes and failings of all the liberal leaders including Juárez complicated the difficult situation.

Between the actual investment of Mexico City on December 25, 1860, and his formal and triumphant entry at the head of 25,000 men on January 1, 1861, Ortega had taken a few natural and emergency actions to restrict looting, to officially publish the Reform Laws, and to provide for interim government.[1] Ocampo, who arrived in the capital ahead of Juárez, issued decrees designed to punish the more serious supporters of the conservative cause and to further implement the Reform Laws.[2] Even so, the basic question of how punitive the government intended to be was still unanswered and the radical elements were already protesting the lack of more drastic action.[3]

On January 10, at Guadalupe, where Juárez spent the night while Ortega made plans for his arrival in the capital, Juárez drafted a proclamation that suggested that he had opted for great leniency in regard to amnesties.[4] It immediately became apparent, however, that a policy of moderation toward the defeated enemy was not going to satisfy public opinion. The case in point proved to be that of Isidro Díaz, Miramón's brother-in-law and principal minister. When most of the ringleaders of the reaction had escaped, Díaz had been captured and on him fell the full fury of public wrath. After first ordering his execution, Juárez commuted the sentence to banishment on the grounds that Díaz had earlier interceded to prevent the execution of Gómez Farías and Degollado. At the same time Juárez decreed a policy of amnesty toward all reactionaries.[5]

Francisco Zarco, editor of the most powerful paper of the liberal party, *El Siglo Diez y Nueve,* raised the alarm. As soon as the rumor of Díaz's pardon and the general amnesty appeared, he wrote, "If this happens, farewell freedom, farewell justice, farewell all public order! . . . It is true that justice can be administered with mercy, and that our Constitution gives the Executive the right to pardon; but that pardon must not be a scandal or a crime against society as a whole."[6] The cry was taken up by the remainder of the press, the political clubs, and the public in general. Zarco continued to attack Juárez. He granted that, in the absence of a congress, the executive had to act independently in many cases for the public good, but that, at the same time, Juárez was overstepping the bounds of necessity. Zarco's primary concern was for the separation of judicial and executive powers. He felt the time had come for the judicial branch of the government to begin operating and that the question of amnesty should be decided by that branch.[7]

Radical opinion had shown no such fine concern over judicial rights, or had perhaps simply recognized executive power when Juárez had moved against representatives of foreign nations. The night before arriving in Mexico City Juárez and his ministers had agreed to expel those representatives of foreign governments who were deemed to have been active in giving aid to the reactionaries. Thus the immediate expulsion of the Papal Nuncio and the Ministers of Spain, Ecuador, and Guatemala had been ordered by Ocampo.[8] When similar action was taken against members of the clergy, however, this added fuel to the fire already blazing over the invasion by the president of the rights of the judiciary.

For their clear support of the conservative government, Juárez ordered the expulsion from Mexico of Lázaro del Garza y Ballesteros, the Archbishop of Mexico, and Bishops Clemente de Jesús Mungía, Joaquín Madrid, Pedro Espinosa, and Pedro Barajas.[9] This action was also denounced by Zarco as a violation of the constitution, and Juan Antonio de la Fuente resigned from the cabinet as a direct result of his disagreement with the order.[10] On the night of January 17, a large meeting was held by several political clubs to protest Juárez's actions. When they failed to receive adequate assurances from Juárez, an indictment of the president was drafted and a resolution adopted calling for a change in the cabinet. By the next night Juárez had canceled the pardon of Díaz and ordered him to stand trial. In addition, on the afternoon of January 17, Ocampo, Llave, Ortega, and Empáran submitted their resignations from the government.[11]

Whatever his motives that had led to such a public outcry,

Juárez realized that he had been mistaken in issuing the pardon for Díaz, but he hoped that its revocation plus the change in the cabinet would quiet criticism.[12] Ignacio Ramírez was called upon to assist in the formation of the cabinet, but discussions took place for three days before the actual announcement of its members could be made. Zarco alleged that the delay resulted from the lack of unity of thought. He declared that the new cabinet should see quite clearly, however, what public opinion demanded.[13] As finally announced on January 21, the new cabinet included Guillermo Prieto, Ortega, Zarco, Ramírez, Pedro Ogazón, and Miguel Auza. The inclusion of Zarco, Ramírez, and Ortega in the new cabinet was clearly an effort to appease public opinion, since these three men were the most popular tribunes of the hour.[14]

This new cabinet was by far the most radical that Juárez was to have. Its program, however, as announced on January 20, involved nothing more radical than the establishment of a constitutional government, the enforcement of the Reform Laws, the guarantee of judicial equality, and the enactment of measures to improve the economy.[15] The major reason for the government's failure to accomplish more of its objectives can certainly be traced to the chronic difficulty with money. Prieto tried diligently for four months to establish a reasonable financial situation, but the problems were too complex and his own ability as an administrator too limited.

The chief source of revenue for the federal government would normally have been the customhouses, but over eighty-five percent of these revenues on the Gulf coast were pledged to pay foreign debts and all of the income on the Pacific coast was pledged. Other taxes had been taken over almost entirely by the governors during the war and, in spite of the entreaties of Prieto, the situation was not improved. The end result was that the government ran a constant monthly deficit and was compelled to borrow from individuals at exorbitant rates of interest. Any other type of loan was impossible until the national credit was improved.

One of the biggest disappointments to the liberal government was the failure of the laws nationalizing church lands to produce more income. The reasons were various. Church property was not as great in value as had often been guessed. Furthermore, much property had been seized by both liberal and conservative leaders during the fighting to meet immediate needs. At the end of 1860 the church was far from poor but one of the best estimates would suggest that the church had lost about 20,000,000 pesos during the Three Years' War.[16] This meant that the amount of property available for alienation was substantially reduced. Added to the reduction was the conflict in the intent and practice of the Ley Lerdo and the July 13, 1859, law. It had been anticipated that a large number of people would become landowners and they in turn would serve as a broad base for the national economy. Unfortunately, the laws had made it possible for land to move into the hands of a few speculators who now attempted to protect their personal interests. Prieto had to somehow harmonize the law "with the social and economic reality which the victorious liberals encountered when they liberated the nation's capital."[17]

On February 5, 1861, a regulatory law was issued in an attempt to clarify titles to land ownership and spell out the form of payment. This latter was necessary because under the previous law the government had begun to grant discounts for payment in cash and had also provided that mortgages could be redeemed for thirty percent cash and sixty percent bonds. In turn, the market for bonds was so poor that they sold at enormous discounts. Thus buyers actually paid as little as twenty percent of the value of ecclesiastical property. While figures are difficult to obtain and interpret it would appear, for example, that during 1861 sales in the Federal District totaled $16,553,147, but in real cash this amounted to only $1,056,424 after bonds and other credits were deducted.[18] Whatever the exact figures, it is clear that the government realized little income from church properties in Mexico City and virtually none reached it from the states. The size of the internal debt was reduced from $53,000,000 in 1856 to $13,000,000 in 1861 but this provided no help in meeting immediate cash needs. It is equally clear that the laws relating to church properties had not had the anticipated social results.

Prieto tried valiantly to solve the economic crisis but by April 22 he left the cabinet to be followed for a few weeks by Mata who had no greater success. Many different methods were tried or discussed. Salaries of public officials were reduced, special loans were levied, reducing the military budget was discussed, and even the extreme measure of obtaining a moratorium on foreign debts so as to release customs revenues for other purposes was once again considered. Before this last critical proposal reached fruition and produced foreign complications, Juárez faced a series of ministerial crises and a variety of political attacks from within his own nation.

As early as November 6, 1860, when the liberal victory had seemed assured, the government had issued a decree calling for special elections in January, 1861, to elect a new congress and a president.[19] The leading candidates for the presidency were Juárez, Ortega, and Lerdo. Lerdo was clearly Juárez's most formidable opponent. He was respected for his financial acumen and his coolness in responsible positions.[20] At the same time there was the growing evidence that the reform laws with which he was primarily identified had failed and that he had been willing to sacrifice the Constitution of 1857 during the war.[21] Whether Lerdo could have defeated Juárez, given Juárez's obvious symbolic if not actual leadership role and the confusing nature of the election machinery, will never be known because he died suddenly in the midst of the election on March 22.[22]

Following the death of Lerdo much of his support rallied around Ortega as a man who was powerful enough to cause Juárez trouble. Ortega already had the support of a large part of the army and a good portion of the revolutionary clubs. He could also depend upon support from many of the newspapers in Mexico.[23] In addition, Doblado, who still had considerable influence, voiced his support of Ortega as early as January.[24] On March 14 Ortega accepted the honorary presidency of the Club Reforma, a powerful club that had been extremely critical of the government.[25] By the end of the month Ortega apparently had decided to step up the criticism of Juárez that had subsided somewhat after the January crisis and thereby indicate his personal antipathy more clearly. Thus, on March 29, the Club Reforma sent a note to Juárez demanding that the entire cabinet be removed and replaced by men who conformed more nearly to their desires and aspirations. This was of course refused by Juárez, but it indicates the limits to which the opposition was willing to go and the strength of political feelings.[26]

Meanwhile the financial plight of the government was providing additional grounds for criticism by the opposition. Prieto considered resigning as early as April 2 and finally did so four days later.[27] Faced with a growing unpopularity because of his association with the government, Ortega demanded that Juárez dismiss Zarco and Ramírez from the cabinet because of their popular disrepute. When this demand was refused, he also resigned.[28] In his letter of resignation Ortega stated that it was clear to him from the attitude of the press and various political circulars that public opinion ran against the cabinet. Since the president had not accepted his proposal, he had no choice but to resign. He concluded with protestations of his respect for legality and the assertion that he would remain at the head of the Division of Zacatecas to sustain democratic institutions.[29]

Juárez accepted the resignation immediately. In answering it for the government, Zarco stated that Ortega had confused public opinion with the noise of a club which possessed no political significance and that he had been moved to act by a minority which had no real political principles. In conclusion he told Ortega that he should await action by the national government on the question of command of the Division of Zacatecas.[30] Ortega's reaction was a blistering attack on the administration. He said that public opinion was against the cabinet because of the large number of laws and decrees that had been issued without careful thought, because the government had demonstrated too much favoritism, and because they had failed to restore peace even in victory. Finally, the government was unpopular because it had failed to listen to public opinion. As for his right to command the Division of Zacatecas, Ortega replied that the force was made up entirely of members of the state national guard and under his exclusive control as governor of Zacatecas. He even pointed to the desire for his removal as being a means to satisfy the personal interests of the government.[31] After another exchange of letters in which Juárez asserted his executive authority over the national guard, he notified Ortega that he had been appointed to command the Division of Zacatecas so that his valuable service would not be lost to the nation now that he was no longer in the cabinet.[32]

For a few days the conflict between Juárez and Ortega caused a great deal of excitement throughout the country. The press commented on it extensively and public demonstrations took place in front of the National Palace and the home of the president.[33] One paper even urged that the people invade the palace and throw the ministers out.[34] Almost without exception, however, the press rallied to the president. Though the disturbance was so far purely ministerial, it was feared that something more drastic would take place. Manuel Zamacona, who had replaced Zarco as editor of *El Siglo Diez y Nueve*, led the way with an editorial asking what had happened to the hero of Capulalpam. He expressed disbelief that this was the same man the country had honored and he felt certain that some evil influences had been brought to bear on him. He urged Ortega to return to the government and the party which he had deserted.[35]

There was still no assurance that order could be preserved. One of the political clubs sent a commission to Juárez to urge him not to accept Ortega's resignation, but Juárez refused to see them after learning the purpose of their visit. The force of Zacatecas approached the stage of pronouncing against the president. The fears of many that violence would result were not realized, however, because of the firmness of Juárez and the failure of Ortega to encourage such violence.[36] The final calming note was struck on May 1 when Ortega issued a manifesto to the Mexican people denying any sanction by him of a revolutionary movement, either by some overt act or by implication. Ortega cautioned that the war was over and the time had come to use the pen and not the sword. He voiced his plans to support the legal government and to do all in his power to reduce the danger of civil war. He concluded by calling upon the Mexican people to have faith in their public officials and solve the nation's problems through legal means.[37]

Though attacks on Juárez continued and there were occasional calls for revolution, the political situation became somewhat more regularized when the newly elected congress met. It was the first meeting of a congress since the days of Comonfort in 1857. Juárez addressed the congress and surrendered his extraordinary powers. Additional cabinet changes were announced and the political dispute entered a new stage.

To divert attention from the political issues, another serious matter began to give cause for concern. As previously stated, the end of the war had not meant the end of conservative opposition. In various parts of the country large bands of former soldiers in the conservative forces continued to attack towns and villages and generally make the roads and highways unsafe. Most of the opposition to these guerrillas had been supplied by the state governors, while the federal government had so far been unable to send out a force which could win a decisive victory over the major reactionary leaders. By the beginning of June the nation became even more conscious of this problem when word reached the capital that Ocampo had been killed by Márquez. He had retired to his ranch in Michocán but was planning to take his seat in congress soon. On May 30 conservative guerrillas captured him though he had been warned they were in the vicinity. They took him to the camp of Márquez and Zuloaga and on June 3 executed him.[38]

The public's reaction was violent and Juárez took steps to protect the lives of conservative prisoners against acts of revenge. Degollado, still not completely cleared of his peacemaking efforts during the war, appeared in a dramatic gesture before congress, asked for and received permission to track down and destroy those who had killed Ocampo. On June 15, however, the "hero of defeats" suffered his last. Conservative troops ambushed him at Salazar, between Mexico City and Toluca, and killed him during the clash that followed.[39] The series of tragedies had still not ended. Five days later, Leandro Valle, "a young man full of hope, laughter, enthusiasm and generous valor,"[40] set out with 800 men to avenge Ocampo and Degollado. Within twenty-four hours he, too, was captured and quickly executed.[41] On June 4, Ortega volunteered his services to seek out and destroy the guerrilla threat, but before the culmination of this military venture his political conflict with Juárez was again of primary significance.[42]

On the same day that Degollado met his unfortunate death, Juárez delivered his inaugural address as the newly-elected president of the republic.[43] The national congress had constituted itself as an electoral college and, after some delay and much argument, had declared Juárez elected on June 11. The vote showed 5,289 for Juárez, 1,989 for Lerdo (who had received votes prior to his death), and 1,846 for Ortega. A total of 512 votes were cast for other candidates. By a close vote of 61–55 the congress approved the majority report declaring Juárez elected and rejected a proposal that the congress choose between Juárez and

Ortega since no candidate had received a majority of the possible electors.[44]

Efforts to block Juárez's continuance in office resumed. As early as May 24 a group of deputies had proposed that the congress create a Committee of Public Safety to administer the government. This had been done but the committee was given no power and was very quickly voted out of existence.[45] Opponents of Juárez then proposed that a triumvirate made up of Doblado, Ortega, and Uraga replace the president, with Juárez, Ogazón, and Degollado as alternates.[46] When this plan was successfully opposed by Juárez, an even clearer move was taken by his opponents to provide for Ortega's succession to the presidency. Congress, on June 27, 1861, elected Ortega as interim president of the Supreme Court and thus next in line for the presidency. Legally the congress had no power to take this step since the power of election was vested in the people, but there was very little opposition since most members of congress apparently believed that some provision should be made in the event of an emergency.[47]

During all of these proceedings Ortega was in the field with an army and there is no evidence that he participated in such actions or even condoned them.[48] Yet it is clear that he opposed Juárez quite seriously and felt that Juárez's position was weak.[49] The American Minister to Mexico, Thomas Corwin, even reported to Secretary of State Seward that not only was every peaceful step being taken to force Juárez out, but also that he thought it would succeed.[50] Clearly Juárez's position was precarious whatever the motives of his opponents. Not only were there radical efforts to remove him, but the problem of conservative guerrillas was far from solved and he could hardly claim to have restored peace to the nation. The perennial financial problem had still to be resolved and foreign problems were building in the background.

Even finding capable and willing associates in the government from among his backers was a problem. After organizing a cabinet in May, Juárez faced another crisis in June with the resignation of several of his ministers. Men like Doblado and Sebastián Lerdo de Tejada were approached but refused to join the government. Not until July was he able to put together another cabinet. It was especially unfortunate that cabinet problems were so serious at a time when such crucial decisions for the nation needed to be made. All through the summer the frequently discussed subject of suspending payments on the foreign and domestic debt was reconsidered. Finally in July, with almost unanimous consent, the cabinet agreed to propose a suspension for two years to congress.[51] Congress accepted the cabinet's proposal and on July 17 passed a law suspending debt service for two years.[52]

Though there had been some discussions with foreign representatives, the exact nature of the decision came as a surprise to the major foreign creditors. Finding no diplomatic way to avoid severe actions, on July 25 the French broke off relations with Mexico and the British suspended them.[53] With the advantage of hindsight it is easy to see that what had happened was simply one step in a sequence of events that seemed almost inevitably to lead to foreign intervention. Yet, given the near bankruptcy of the Juárez government, the only real question is perhaps whether the debt suspension should have taken place much earlier.

The immediate recommendation of the Spanish and French representatives for intervention was not the first time there had been activities aimed at European influence in Mexico. At first Spain led the way in urging an active policy. The hope of some renewed relationship with her one-time province had always been cherished in Spain, and the present situation appeared to offer possibilities. In 1846 there had been suggestions on the part of the Spanish government that intervention might be necessary to establish a firm government in Mexico. In September, 1861, the United States was informed that Spain was about to make war upon Mexico to secure redress for damages and insults. Faced with a war of its own, the United States government stated that no objections to such a war would be made if it did not infringe upon the rights of the United States and did not have the acquisition of territory or the subversion of the republican government of Mexico as its object.

With the U.S. Civil War in mind, Spain moved to interest Napoleon III in some enterprise. In France, meanwhile, there were already important forces moving that country toward intervention. A group of Mexican refugees had been attempting for some time to spread the gospel of monarchy for Mexico.[54] The most outstanding members of this small group were José Manuel Hidalgo y Esnaurrizar, a young diplomat; J. M. Gutiérrez de Estrada, a long-time monarchist and exile; and Juan N. Almonte, the former Minister to France for the Miramón government. These men had taken advantage of the Empress Eugenie's interest in politics to urge the creation of a Mexican empire as an ally of France or even as a protectorate. These efforts had the desired effect on Napoleon who was also being urged to intervene by his Minister to Mexico, Pierre de Saligny.

Comte de Saligny, as the representative of important French financial circles, was interested not only in intervention but a complete change in the Mexican system of government. He had become financially involved with Napoleon's brother, the Duc de Morny, in obtaining a favorable payment on the Jecker bonds. Morny was "one of those great lords, at once statesman and libertine, so frequent in French history, and he concealed an insatiable appetite for money, pleasures, and honors beneath the exquisite manners of a punctilious, nonchalant, and very elegant prince."[55] Morny was a strong ally of the interventionists at court and Saligny, though he recognized the Juárez government, seized frequent opportunities to pressure it and misrepresented the situation to France when he thought it to his advantage. As a result of these various factors, the Spanish proposal found a ready reception in France. Napoleon, in turn, moved to obtain England's consent to participate in joint intervention.

The British government was willing to enter into the project provided it was understood that there should be no interference with the right of the Mexican people to select their own government. This point of view was incorporated into a convention drawn up by representatives of the three nations at London on October 31, 1861. Actually, the British government was unofficially aware of Napoleon's long-range plans for the establishment of a monarchy in Mexico, but on paper, at least, the British terms had been accepted. The London convention provided, in essence, for consultation among the three powers with the object of organizing an expedition to occupy the ports of Mexico in an effort to force collection of the debts owed to those powers by Mexico. The United States was invited to participate, but refused.[56]

José Antonio de la Fuente, who represented Mexico in Paris, took immediate steps there to forestall the possible intervention. In a note to the French Foreign Minister, Edouard Antoine Thouvenel, he explained in some detail the circumstances that had forced Mexico into the temporary expediency of postponing debt payments. He assured Thouvenel that the situation was not as bad as it might appear and urged him to await the complete facts of the situation, implying clearly that Saligny was not telling the whole story. The effort by De la Fuente was fruitless because Thouvenel replied bluntly that his government had confidence in Saligny.[57]

Although France could not be made to change her direction, there still remained the possibility that the United States would act in some fashion to prevent intervention or, failing that, provide assistance in repelling would-be invaders. There was no question that the United States government was sympathetic to the republican cause in Mexico and that the still ill-defined Monroe Doctrine placed the United States in a position of opposing outside influences. There was the further fact that the Confederate government had been toying with various possibilities that would provide Mexican assistance against the Union. Nonetheless, the existence of the American Civil War prevented the United States from taking steps it might otherwise have taken. Secretary of State Seward at least suggested to Minister Corwin that the United States government might be willing to pay the interest on the Mexican debt for three years and take a lien on public lands in Lower California, Chihuahua, Sonora, and Sinaloa as a lien. Seward hoped that he could obtain approval in general of such an approach from the Senate in advance of any agreement, but he was unable to do so.[58]

Even without senatorial approval, negotiations continued, and all the while Seward tried to get British and French agreement to postpone intervention. Finally Corwin negotiated a treaty with Mexico that provided for United States payment of interest for five years provided hostilities were not undertaken. As protection the United States was to receive a lien on the lands and mineral rights in the states mentioned earlier. A default clause was inserted, making the territory United States property at the end of six years of nonpayment by Mexico. Whatever the good intention that lay behind the agreement, and it would appear that the motivation was somewhat less devious than earlier United States negotiations with Mexico, the treaty was opposed in most quarters in both countries. The United States Senate flatly rejected the treaty and the possibility of American private loans to Mexico was explored but to no avail.

Because of the failure of any American effort to prevent intervention and the failure of negotiations in both France and England, it became Juárez's unpleasant duty to announce the decision made in the Treaty of London for intervention. In anticipation of the arrival of Spanish ships already in Havana, the government issued orders to check on defenses at Veracruz and other ports.[59] Even as late as October 30, however, the Juárez government had hopes that further negotiations with the British might still head off intervention. They did not know the terms of the London convention and did not realize that even a settlement with the British would not bring the desired results. There is even an indication that due to faulty communications or ineptness the British Minister to Mexico, Sir Charles Wyke, was unaware of how far the British government had committed itself.

For several weeks Manuel M. Zamacona, Mexico's Foreign Minister, had been negotiating with Wyke.[60] Wyke proved to be a very tough bargainer and managed to exact from Zamacona a virtual return to the *status quo ante* for the British. This meant the immediate repayment of money stolen from the British legation by Miramón and from the silver train by Doblado. It also meant the resumption of interest payments to bondholders from customs revenue and the assignment of still new revenue for payment on claims arising out of the civil war. Most insulting of all, the treaty allowed British officials to examine the books of the customhouses to ensure good faith, and British agents were given exclusive rights to sell special treasury certificates to foreign exporters.[61]

For obvious reasons Juárez was hesitant about accepting the treaty and it was not signed until November 21. Zamacona thought that he had correctly assessed the mood of congress but, largely due to the efforts of Lerdo, the treaty was rejected. Lerdo argued, and a majority agreed, that the treaty went too far in sacrificing Mexican sovereignty.[62] At the same time, the congress repealed parts of the July 17 law as it applied to the British and agreed to resume payments on foreign debts.[63] Thus, oddly enough, though the British had in fact obtained all that they wished, Wyke insisted that the treaty be ratified or he would be compelled to leave. When his request was denied, Wyke requested his passport and left Mexico City on December 16 en route to London, only to arrive in Veracruz and find that he had been named representative of the British for the intervention.

Actually, most Mexicans were unaware of or unconcerned about the possible foreign intervention until about the time of the Wyke-Zamacona negotiations. Political debate was still more concerned with internal differences than the external threat. Indeed, whatever concern was expressed was simply in criticism of the ineptness of the Juárez administration. Old charges of softness in his treatment of reactionaries were repeated. Incompetence of ministers was alleged, the insolence of the clergy was pointed out, and the dictatorial nature of the government in the absence of individual guarantees was decried.[64]

Some criticisms of the administration were perhaps warranted, but it is clear that no president of Mexico at the time would have escaped criticism. Certainly efforts had been and were being made to correct the difficulties the civil war had left behind. In one area a degree of success was achieved. On July 2, 1861, Ortega had left the capital once again in pursuit of Márquez and, though he quarreled constantly with the government over the adequacy or inadequacy of the supplies he was furnished, early in August a decisive encounter took place.[65] Ortega located Márquez, Zuloaga, and several other conservative leaders with about 2,500 men at Jalatlaco. Porfirio Díaz, serving under Ortega, attacked without orders and defeated and dispersed the reactionary forces after being joined by the remainder of Ortega's command.[66] News of the victory was received jubilantly in Mexico City. Salvos of artillery were fired and public demonstrations were held. Though the victory was still only a temporary relief from conservative attacks, it did come at a time when good news was badly needed.[67]

Even a victory produced further political problems for Juárez. Jalatlaco increased the reputation of Ortega, around whom opposition to Juárez still centered. While the search for Márquez had been going on, several supporters of Ortega in Mexico City notified him that there were indications of a move on the part of former president Comonfort to reestablish himself in the presidency and that the time had come for Ortega to make a move.[68] He was also advised that Juárez expected him to be defeated and thus eliminated as a political opponent.[69] Though nothing had come of this, Ortega could hardly appear publicly without some criticism of Juárez being implied. Thus when Ortega appeared before the permanent deputation of congress on August 20 to officially assume his post as president of the court, his speech attracted considerable attention.

In his speech Ortega spoke primarily in generalities but he did warn against the possibility of military victories without practical results. He also intimated that the government was too concerned with punishing the few reactionaries who remained and was not trying to put into practice the principles of the reform.[70] While much of the press argued that there was no hidden meaning in Ortega's speech, the opposition to Juárez continued to be active and to associate Ortega's name with its activities.[71]

On September 3, shortly after the opening of an extraordinary session of congress, a congressional committee urged Juárez to dismiss his cabinet. After his refusal, on September 7, a petition signed by fifty-one deputies requested that Juárez resign since he had failed to advance the reform program and had fallen into disrepute in the eyes of the people. Though the petition did not mention Ortega's name, it was generally understood that he would become acting president. On the same day, however, another petition, signed by fifty-two members of congress, voiced confidence in the administration and expressed the belief that, even though errors had been made, Juárez's resignation was no answer to the problems.[72]

Still another event indicative of the relation between Ortega and Juárez took place at about the same time that the congressional petitions appeared. On August 23, Ortega was asked to take over a military command against Mejía and other conservative leaders who were still operating in the mountains north of Mexico City. Ortega accepted the command and obtained permission to absent himself from the Supreme Court. During the next few days he argued with the Secretary of War about money and resources needed for the campaign. On the same day that the congressional committee had asked Juárez to dismiss his cabinet, he had a strong argument with Juárez over the subject. Juárez implied that hard work and not a large army was needed. On September 9, after his demands had not been met, Ortega advised the government that he could not accept the command and be responsible for the outcome of the campaign.[73] On the following day Ortega's resignation was accepted with the comment that even if his demands had not been met, there had been sufficient resources to carry out the campaign.[74]

On September 12, Doblado was named commander-in-chief and instructed to assume Ortega's role.[75] At the same time Zaragoza ordered Ortega to turn over the forces of Zacatecas to General Francisco Alatorre. Ortega protested that he had not resigned the command and that, as governor of the state, he had the right and duty to retain it.[76] Ortega also wrote to Doblado expressing his confusion over this order and asking for assistance. Doblado replied that he could only follow orders but would do what he could.[77] Ortega was moving his forces to Querétaro when he received orders from Juárez to proceed to Zacatecas and turn the command over to Alatorre.[78]

The situation remained critical until Doblado apparently successfully intervened and conciliated Juárez, because on October 2, Ortega was named second-in-command under Doblado.[79] Thus the fear that Ortega was holding on to an army to move against the government was dissipated and a major threat to Juárez was removed. Ortega himself apparently failed to take the field, however, and returned to his position on the court. Elements under Santiago Tapía and Porfirio Díaz did, however, contact and defeat Márquez and Zuloaga later in October near Pachuca.

With the reduction of the guerrilla menace and the temporary truce with Ortega, Juárez should have had a reasonably united government behind him when facing the immediate threat of foreign intervention, but such was not the case. On October 9 and 10 anti-*juarista* members of congress again tried to force cabinet changes on Juárez. Juárez took the position that, as chief executive, he could not give in to congressional demands, especially what he considered a minority view, without destroying the nature of the government. Unfortunately for Juárez, a cabinet change did become necessary. After congress refused to accept the Wyke-Zamacona Treaty, Zamacona resigned.[80] In the days that followed, Juárez tried without success to get several persons to assume the leadership of the ministry. Since Lerdo had led the fight against the treaty and was developing into a strong leader, he would have been a logical person for the post, but he also refused.[81] Characteristic of much of Mexican politics, the problem between Lerdo and Juárez was more a question of persons to serve in the cabinet rather than a question of issues.[82] Juárez finally turned to Doblado.[83]

In the discussions between Doblado and Juárez much of the difficulty with the Mexican political system was brought to light. Doblado asked for complete freedom in the selection of ministers, arguing for a system of ministerial responsibility and independence more like the political systems of Europe. Juárez, on the other hand, maintained that the Mexican constitution placed responsibility for policy in the president and he could not abdicate either the responsibility or the power to name and remove ministers. Though neither Juárez nor Doblado convinced the other of his view, some agreement was reached after Juárez approved the cabinet members Doblado intended to name and a new ministry was formed.[84] Doblado immediately asked congress to grant the executive extraordinary powers to insure the preservation of national independence and the reform laws. The request was granted on December 11, just four days before congress closed its sessions.[85] At the same time the suspension of individual guarantees was continued.

An emergency indeed did exist because the threatened invasion became a fact on December 14, 1861, when the Spanish contingent of 6,000 men arrived at Veracruz. They landed immediately and on January 9 the French squadron arrived, bringing with it 2,000 marines and some 600 zouaves. The English landed only 800 marines, an indication of their reserve even though they had signed the London Convention.

The commissioners of the three intervening powers met at Veracruz to outline their claims and determine a course of action. The English and Spanish representatives made quite moderate claims but it was obvious that the French were attempting to impose impossible conditions on the Mexican government. Saligny, in view of his own and his sovereign's far-reaching plans, was completely opposed to an understanding with the Juárez government. The English and Spanish representatives denounced the French claims as unjustified and incapable of fulfillment, and the meeting ended in discord. Something had to be done, however, as the weather in Veracruz was notorious. A large number of the troops were already hospitalized with fever. The commissioners therefore sent word to Juárez that they wished a meeting aimed at allowing the troops to be moved inland.

Still hoping to head off hostilities, Juárez agreed to a conference and selected Doblado to represent his government. The meeting took place on February 19 at La Soledad, near Veracruz. General Juan Prim, the commander of the Spanish forces and an enlightened professional soldier married to the niece of Juárez's Minister of Finance, served as the spokesman for the allies. It was agreed at this conference that the invading troops would be allowed to move to Córdoba, Orizaba, and Tehuacán, three spots higher up in the mountains toward Mexico City. In return the allies promised, as Juárez had insisted, that the liberal government was in effect recognized and that the invaders had no plans to attack the independence and sovereignty of Mexico. The Soledad Agreement, signed on February 19 and approved by Juárez four days later, further provided that formal negotiations would be held on April 15, at Orizaba.

Whether by luck or foresight, Juárez was wise to postpone the actual negotiations because in the interim the differences between the allied commissioners increased and France's position became more transparent. The commissioners met on April 9 and, as had been expected, an immediate clash of violently opposed views resulted. For the English and Spanish it was merely a question of how to arrange a dignified exit for their governments. Saligny now openly advocated the policy of intervention desired by Napoleon III, in opposition to the agreement made at La Soledad. Under these circumstances an agreement was impossible. On April 11 the allies notified the Mexican government that the London Convention had been dissolved and that the Spanish and English forces would withdraw. The French would retire to the coast and begin action about April 20. This last move by the French was to be made under the terms of the Soledad Agreement, which had provided that if no satisfactory settlement were made, all troops would be marched back to the coast before beginning any aggressive action.[86]

Juárez replied to Wyke and Prim that the Mexican government was prepared to negotiate a settlement with them, and Wyke requested that Doblado represent him. Juárez instructed Doblado to renegotiate the substance of the Wyke-Zamacona treaty with changes making it more acceptable to Mexico.[87] Clearly Juárez still felt that an agreement could be reached that did not include the insulting provision for British inspection of Mexican customhouses and for the setting aside of funds sufficient to appease the demands of both France and Spain. The British turned out to be as obstinate as ever in their demands and the treaty that Doblado finally signed was even stronger than the earlier one. It obviously stood no chance of ratification and Wyke left for home with British claims still unsatisfied. Even as hopes for more British sympathy faded, the possibility of substantial aid from the United States still remained dim. Secretary Seward saw advantages to a loan by the United States to Mexico but the same objections as before were raised and the United States Senate refused to go along.[88]

Meanwhile, the government had been extremely active in preparing for the possible advent of hostilities. Juárez had addressed the nation at the time of the Spanish arrival, pointing out the pretexts Spain might have to wage war on Mexico, and summoning all citizens to the defense of their country. Although most of the interior states were still having internal troubles, a steady stream of troops began coming from them to the capital. Some of the conservative leaders offered their services to the liberal government out of a spirit of nationalism, but the major reactionary leaders, Mejía, Márquez, and Zuloaga, stepped up activities and generally aided the cause of the intervention. Juárez declared a state of siege in several states, levied new and emergency taxes to raise funds, and, when the French military move became a reality, provided stiff penalties for any Mexican who remained in areas under French occupation or in any way aided the French.[89]

Hostilities had actually begun between the French and Mexicans in April. Additional troops had been landed under the command of General Carlos Laurencez and on April 16 a proclamation issued by the French announced them as liberals with the purpose of pacifying the nation. On April 19, General Almonte, who had returned to Mexico under French auspices, issued a proclamation to the Mexican people urging support of the intervention, and some areas under strong clerical influence declared for Almonte as chief of the republic. Shortly thereafter a French declaration named Almonte president, and on April 20 French forces occupied Orizaba, taking advantage of a technicality in the Soledad Agreement to ignore their obligation to return to the coast before commencing hostilities.[90]

The first objective of the French was the city of Puebla, about halfway between Orizaba and Mexico City. The city was defended by a force under the command of Zaragoza, who had distinguished himself during the War of the Reform. Laurencez made the mistake of expecting an easy victory and also chose one of the worst possible spots to attack. On May 5 the day-long attack on Puebla was made and the unskilled Mexican soldiers decisively defeated the three French attacks up the hill leading to a strongly fortified outpost of the city. Zaragoza and Díaz, who was a subordinate officer at Puebla, won fame for themselves and Mexico.[91] In the capital there was much rejoicing and perhaps some surprise at the tremendous victory, and the anniversary of this battle became one of the great national holidays.

Zaragoza now made plans to push the French back to the coast from Orizaba, to where they had withdrawn following their defeat at Puebla. He had received reinforcements of men and money when Ortega joined him at Puebla on June 2, 1862.[92] Shortly after his arrival on the scene, Ortega took it upon himself to find some way to avoid further hostilities. On June 10 he wrote to Saligny and explained that Mexico was pro-republican and would not tolerate a monarchy. He very naively asked if it would not look better in history if the issues at stake were settled by diplomacy rather than by war.[93] Although Ortega took this action without the knowledge of Juárez or Zaragoza, he apparently had been taught a lesson about letter writing by Juárez, because he advised the president of his action. Juárez very politely advised Ortega to confine himself to military matters and expressed the hope that the letter to Saligny had not hindered operations against the French. Temporarily subdued and having received an unsatisfactory answer from Saligny, Ortega assured Juárez that the proposal had been in strict confidence and no embarrassment to the government should result.[94]

On June 13, Zaragoza launched his planned attack on Orizaba

in the hope of following up the advantage that Puebla had given him. Unfortunately for Zaragoza, the French successfully surprised Ortega, who had been assigned the task of defending the heights overlooking the city, and drove him off. Consequently, when Zaragoza attacked with his main forces without knowledge of Ortega's defeat, he was driven back from Orizaba. The French failed to pursue his forces, however, and retired to Orizaba. Zaragoza's forces then retreated to Puebla where they remained inactive for the next few months. The French concentrated on fortifying Orizaba and their other gains along the coast.[95] The failure to take Orizaba was unfortunate but it was still to be a year before the French were able to launch another attack on Puebla.

Even in the face of foreign intervention, Juárez's political opponents refused to give him respite from their attacks. Perhaps the victory at Puebla gave them a feeling of overconfidence or perhaps there was some unconscious death wish, but the internecine quarrels continued until the end of the French intervention. Radicals had claimed all along that Juárez was too easy in his treatment of reactionaries and when members of the church hierarchy actively supported the French, new cries for restrictions on the clergy were heard. Although some had already been issued, more were demanded. By August Juárez gave in, and a law was issued making it a crime to preach against the government and prohibiting the wearing of ecclesiastical garb in public. This was followed by restrictions on religious demonstrations outside the churches and finally, in February, 1863, by the disbanding of most convents in Mexico.[96]

Not only radicals but independent governors still existed. The intransigence of Vidaurri in Nuevo León had plagued Juárez in the past and would in the future. In July Juárez wrote to Vidaurri pleading for money and supplies. In spite of the fact that Vidaurri had more cash than most officials and in spite of the fact that he had a constant source of income from Confederate goods moving through his state, he refused to cooperate.[97]

In the midst of political and military crises Juárez was the victim of personal tragedy as well. In July his infant daughter Amada died and later in the same month his wife's father and his old patron died also.[98] It seems Juárez was as well endowed with the stoic virtues of his Indian ancestry as his partisans claimed for him. Surely cabinet crises were becoming easier to weather all the time, and it is just as well because one came in August.

Doblado, who had avoided major opposition better than most leading political figures of the time, felt that he had become anathema to many of the leading liberals and could only cause the administration harm, thus his resignation.[99] Juárez agreed and accepted the resignation although there were also rumors that Juárez had pressured Doblado into resigning because he was suspected of being willing to do away with Juárez and compromise the Constitution in order to avoid further hostilities.[100] Whatever the truth of the matter, Doblado's resignation came as a surprise to most. Within a few days, however, De la Fuente took over the leadership of the cabinet and Doblado was given command of the forces operating in the interior against Mejía.[101] The cabinet change failed to satisfy liberals in the capital, and attacks were again launched on Juárez and the new cabinet.

On September 8, the liberals suffered still another blow when Zaragoza died of typhoid fever. Ortega was named to succeed him as head of the army of the west.[102] Whatever Juárez may have thought of Ortega's political opposition, he recognized the general's military abilities and was wise enough to make use of them at this critical time. Ortega immediately set to work building up the defenses around the city of Puebla and by November believed that they were almost invincible.[103]

Juárez's amazing ability to present himself as a symbol of the nation was both demonstrated and tested after Ortega undertook the defenses at Puebla. Fréderic Forey, who had recently replaced Laurencez as French commander, wrote Ortega to thank him for returning some prisoners after the May 5 battle and assured him that he considered him a brave soldier. However, he added, he could not correspond with the government of Mexico without repugnance and he hoped that Ortega would be working for a better cause in the near future.[104] Before responding, Ortega sought Juárez's advice. Juárez advised Ortega to answer that he considered Forey insulting not to the person of Juárez but to the government of Mexico.[105] Ortega did so and told Forey that the true interests of France did not lie in cooperating with a few discontented persons to overthrow a government supported by the Mexican people. Furthermore, he wished Forey to understand that, aside from his personal regard for Juárez, he was serving his country freely. He concluded by returning Forey's letter stating that it had no place among his records.[106]

Meanwhile preparations at Puebla continued. Juárez visited the city to review the army and inspect the fortifications as well as provide the morale boost needed at such a time. Though Ortega requested a unified command under either Comonfort or himself, Juárez had decided to retain independent armies, perhaps because he had reason to distrust both generals a bit.[107] At last, on February 23, Forey began to move in the direction of Puebla. The actual fighting began on March 21 and soon developed into a siege.[108] Lack of coordination between the Mexican armies plus the determination of the French finally decided the outcome, however, and on May 17 the city surrendered. The Mexican historian José M. Vigil has summed up the results at Puebla quite well. He wrote: "After a siege of sixty-two days the valiant defenders of Puebla succumbed, not to the arms of a powerful enemy but to the horrors of hunger and the lack of munitions of war. A town had been lost, but the honor of Mexico had been saved."[109] Though the French took many prisoners, including Ortega and a number of generals, hundreds of them managed to escape before they could be shipped to France. Fortunately, Ortega, Díaz, and others who still had much to contribute to the military support of Juárez, were among those who escaped.

Regardless of how much honor had been saved at Puebla, there were serious doubts that the capital could be held. Though the issue was debated both then and later, Juárez decided the city could not be held and plans were made for its evacuation. Congress in almost its last session voted Juárez extraordinary powers to last for the duration of the war. Even this was, strangely enough, debated at great length.[110] Congress also ordered the chief federal authorities to transfer the government to San Luis Potosí. Thus, on May 31, Juárez, accompanied by the greater part of the public officials, left the capital.[111] On his arrival in San Luis Potosí, he issued a proclamation setting forth the reasons for abandoning the capital and sent circulars to the various state governors giving them authority to act in certain cases without instructions from the federal government. A reorganization of the cabinet was also announced.[112]

CHAPTER V

The Empire and Its End

WITH JUÁREZ IN RETREAT, THE FRENCH OCCUPIED MEXICO CITY in the first part of June, 1863. There Forey, after a staged welcome for the conquering forces, decreed the selection of a supreme council of thirty-five members, which in turn named a governing board of three men led by Almonte. This council then called a convention of two hundred and fifteen so-called notables which on July 8, in accordance with the plans of Napoleon III, pronounced itself in favor of establishing a monarchy, with a moderate, hereditary Catholic prince to be given the title of "Emperor of Mexico." At the same time the crown was offered to Maximilian, archduke of Austria, with the proviso that should he decline, Napoleon would name an alternate. Until the establishment of the monarchy, the triumvirate would govern as a regency.[1]

In addition to these political steps, the French set about consolidating their military position. By the first of August, the imperialists held over sixty towns and hamlets between Veracruz and Mexico City and controlled a circuit of at least twenty-five leagues around the capital. Two months later the actual gains were not much greater, but fighting was going on in all the central provinces from Jalisco and San Luis Potosí into Oaxaca.[2]

Juárez, in the face of the French advance, managed to sustain his government in San Luis Potosí for almost seven months. Time was needed to obtain armies and the funds to maintain them. Men to fight could be found easily enough although their quality as compared to professional soldiers left much to be desired. Supplying them was a different matter and as in the earlier War of the Reform, finances would be a perennial problem. Juárez came to feel during the weeks at San Luis Potosí and during the peregrinations of his government during the next four years that the only sure, consistent thing that represented the republican cause was the symbol of the president and the constitutional foundation upon which the government rested. Whether he was defending Juárez, the man, or Juárez, President of Mexico, had been an issue almost since the day he had assumed power. During the earlier three years of conflict there had been honest liberals who had felt that the removal of Juárez from the presidency would have hastened victory. This feeling would continue throughout the Intervention. Even without the issue of peace, there had been, and would continue to be, those who felt that Juárez was inept or insufficiently active, that he was too conservative or had become so, that he had lost public confidence or had never had it, and that he was too dictatorial and refused to allow the judiciary or the legislature to assume its rightful powers. It was thus in the days at San Luis Potosí and the dark days that followed. Perhaps it was Juárez's very stubbornness in the face of attacks, the tenaciousness with which he argued for legal processes, that in the long run gave the Mexican nation its feeling of confidence in the man. Certainly, it endeared him to a people in retrospect and frustrated his opponents during his lifetime.

Perhaps the biggest specific political problem facing Juárez in June, 1863, was the split between radicals and moderates. The former feared Doblado while the latter pressured Juárez to reorganize his cabinet to include Doblado as its leader. Juárez, as had become characteristic, resisted the pressures for a change, arguing that he would have had a new cabinet every month for the past five years if he had given in to all such pressures.[3] On August 14, however, a change was forced by the resignation of Terán and Juárez tried to appease Doblado with a minor position in the cabinet. Doblado refused and Juárez was forced to make him head of the cabinet. The two then argued over the composition of the cabinet for two days before agreement was reached.[4] The result was a cabinet composed of Doblado, Lerdo, Comonfort, and Nuñez.

The relief was brief for Juárez. Within two days Doblado attacked Zamacona and Zarco, with whom he had had a long personal feud, by attempting to cut off government funds paid them for publishing official newspapers. He also ordered them to leave the country within a month. Juárez intervened to protect them on the grounds that they enjoyed congressional immunity as members of the permanent delegation of congress that remained in existence even when congress was not in session. Doblado appeared to accept the decision but continued his pressure on Juárez to the point that a confrontation occurred and Doblado threatened to resign. Juárez accepted the resignation on September 7 and once again had to pick a cabinet. He persuaded Comonfort and Lerdo not to resign and selected Iglesias to join Nuñez in the new cabinet headed by Lerdo. Lerdo and Iglesias were to join Juárez as the only continuing civilian officials throughout the Intervention.[5]

Political problems with politicians are to be expected but the administration now faced essentially political problems with the military leaders upon whom any defense against the French depended. The republican army, which had become quite disorganized by this time, was divided into five divisions under the direction of Minister of War Comonfort. The eastern division consisted of about 3,000 men and was under the command of Porfirio Díaz, who operated virtually independently of the rest of the army. Another division of over 4,000 men and considerable resources was located in Guanajuato under Doblado, who had returned there after leaving the cabinet. Other divisions of about the same size were under Ortega and José López Uraga in Zacatecas and Michoacán respectively. Berriozábal was placed in command of a reserve division.[6] In Durango, Governor Patoni was actively providing resources with the cooperation of republican leaders in Chihuahua and Sinaloa. Troops were also being raised in Puebla and Tlaxcala as well as other locations where the opportunity existed. Clearly some unification of command, especially in the center where the French were most active, was needed. Lerdo worked with Comonfort to try to persuade Uraga to accept a command, but Uraga refused on the grounds that he would be unable to get enough money and men to succeed and his reputation would suffer. Efforts by Juárez to force the issue failed and the divided command continued.[7]

So long as Juárez's armies, however uncoordinated, existed and so long as the semblance of a government could be maintained, there was still hope for a negotiated end to the Intervention or, at least, assistance in the fight for independence from outside. Diplomatic agents were active wherever possible to remind friendly nations that Juárez was still the legitimate head of the

Mexican government.[8] Matías Romero worked diligently in the United States to increase and improve the small flow of arms that reached Mexico in spite of the Civil War.[9] To assist in these diplomatic efforts Juárez tried vainly until as late as December to assemble congress.[10] Even after he had given up and resigned himself simply to the existence of a permanent deputation, there were occasional conversations about the desirability of a congress.

Part of the reason a congress was needed had nothing to do with appearances. There had always been those who charged that Juárez acted too independently without relying on the other branches of government. Obviously, without a legislative branch it was more difficult to avoid such a charge. Perhaps out of necessity Juárez had already made one undiplomatic move. On November 28, 1863, while still at San Luis Potosí, he had exercised the extraordinary powers conferred on him to declare that the terms of existing Supreme Court justices expired in December. This meant that only Ortega would continue to serve since his term ran until June, 1868. Juárez also had announced that he would name successors even before November.[11] Some liberal leaders felt that Juárez's actions failed to comply with the constitutional division of powers and used this as another charge against him. Obviously, some of this opposition was based on personal jealousy and rivalry but it unfortunately coincided with serious military reverses that could also be used to discredit the chief executive.

The French had taken little military action during the late summer rainy season, although political activity had increased. Maximilian, who had been offered the throne on October 3, 1863, demanded a popular election to determine the wishes of the Mexican people. The fact that such an election might be and actually was a farce, never seems to have occurred to the Austrian prince. The idea seemed desirable to Napoleon, however, for the possible effect it might have on diplomatic relations with other nations, especially the United States. A campaign was begun to get an expression of approval from the interior towns of Mexico for a monarchy. The French government recalled Forey and Saligny, whose dual control of the expedition had proven slow and unsatisfactory, and placed General F. A. Bazaine in complete control of the French forces. Under his direction as many elections as could be held, or were thought necessary, took place with the expected results transmitted to Maximilian.

Bazaine also reorganized the command of the French armies and sought to enlist further aid from those Mexicans who could be convinced that the Intervention was desirable. By the beginning of November, the French forces numbered about 34,700 men with 14,000 of them mobilized to begin operations at the end of the rainy season.[12] Before the outcome of the campaign could be known Bazaine was not opposed to accomplishing his aims by diplomatic rather than military means. Working through a moderate liberal in Mexico City, he sent a representative to meet with Lerdo. Lerdo made it clear that he could negotiate only with the understanding that Mexico's independence and right to choose her own form of government were respected. By the time Bazaine received this reply his own military fortunes had improved to the point that he, in turn, insisted that negotiations depended on the acceptance of the Intervention. Clearly there was no room for further discussion and the peace effort ended.[13]

The fighting in November and December were in fact quite favorable to the French. Querétaro and Morelia were taken in November and San Miguel Allende, Guanajuato, León, and Lagos were among the more important towns taken by the two French armies in the same month. These successes seriously endangered the city of San Luis Potosí; on December 22, with the army of Mejía approaching, Juárez and his government abandoned that point and moved to the more distant Saltillo, capital of the state of Coahuila. Monterrey was considered, but the doubtful attitude of Vidaurri and the rumors of negotiations between him and the imperialists made that location seen inadvisable.[14] Even before Juárez reached Saltillo the French occupied San Luis Potosí and a little over a week later seized the major city of Guadalajara.

Juárez arrived in Saltillo on January 9 with still another reshuffling of his cabinet. This change was caused by the departure of Nuñez and the death of Comonfort in a brief skirmish in November.[15] The usual political criticism of his cabinet could be expected and, with the disastrous turn of events militarily, still new and more drastic steps were taken to remove Juárez. It is understandable that some supporters of the republican cause might sincerely have believed that Juárez the man was still the obstacle to a negotiated settlement, but there is no evidence that this was in fact the case. The earlier exchange between Lerdo and Bazaine would bear out such a contention. Nonctheless, Ortega and Doblado now took the lead in arguing just such a point of view.

On January 14, a commission representing Ortega, Doblado, and J. María Chávez, the governor of Aguascalientes, called on Juárez and asked that he resign.[16] The commissioners argued that the French would not negotiate with Juárez and thus he should resign. They assured him, however, that his decision would be obeyed. Juárez naturally refused the request, pointing out that the quarrel of the French was not with him personally but with the form of government. In addition, Juárez asserted that he had a duty to the Mexican people and to appearance to remain in office.[17] In stating to Doblado his reasons for not resigning, Juárez added that there was no assurance that the enemy would treat with Ortega, whom they considered as a man who had gone back on his word. For that matter Juárez doubted they would treat with anyone who would not accept the Intervention.[18] The firmness of Juárez prevailed with Doblado and Ortega. Both remained loyal and soon were called upon by Juárez for assistance.

When Juárez had moved to Saltillo he had realized that Monterrey was a better location, but Vidaurri's lack of cooperation was well known and his forces were too great for the government to safely risk challenging. By February, however, Mejía had seized Matehuala and San Luis Potosí, and Ortega had abandoned Zacatecas and Fresnillo. Saltillo was clearly threatened. Thus Juárez decided to force the issue. Through his Minister of Finance he demanded that Vidaurri turn over to the federal government the sources of revenue in the states he controlled.

Vidaurri declared that the states could not spare these revenues and forbade the customhouse collectors to pay over any funds to Juárez. The latter responded by announcing that he planned to move the federal government to Monterrey. On February 12, Doblado's troops were sent ahead to Monterrey and a few hours later Juárez followed. Upon arriving at Doblado's encampment, Juárez learned that Vidaurri had seized cannons as if intended for use in a demonstration upon Juárez's arrival.[19] Vidaurri reinforced his troops and demanded the withdrawal of Doblado although he stated his willingness to have the government remain. A situation approaching hostilities continued for two days until Juárez and his advisers held a brief conference with Vidaurri. The meeting almost resulted in a declaration of revolt against Juárez and he hastily withdrew his troops back to Saltillo.[20]

Having suffered a serious embarrassment as well as a real threat, Juárez now decided to act as he had known for some time he must if Vidaurri could not be won over. Specifically, he had to be eliminated.[21] Juárez turned to Ortega and others to bring their forces to Saltillo to assist Doblado.[22] He sent secret agents into the state to work against the governor and declared the union of Coahuila and Nuevo León dissolved and both states in a state of siege. Though Vidaurri announced elections to determine the wishes of the people, Juárez issued a decree declaring Vidaurri a traitor and all who participated in the election also traitors.[23] Vidaurri, seeing that Juárez was imperiling his own private little empire, considered entering into negotiations with Bazaine, but when he realized Juárez's strength he attempted to reach an agreement. Juárez held out for unconditional surrender and Vidaurri consequently abandoned Monterrey and fled to Texas.[24] Vidaurri later defected to the French but he was no good to them and was at least no longer a problem to Juárez.

On April 2 Juárez moved his government to Monterrey while republican forces held the French temporarily in San Luis Potosí. Thus when the time approached for Maximilian to assume the throne that he had accepted on April 10, the ground held by the imperialist forces was considerable. The most important parts of the country had been brought under their control although republican guerrillas still operated in many areas, especially Michoacán, Jalisco, and Puebla. The republicans still held the rather scantily inhabited provinces of Sinaloa, Sonora, Durango, Chihuahua, Nuevo León, and part of Tamaulipas. In the south they occupied Guerrero, Oaxaca, Tabasco, and Chiapas, where Díaz had been unusually successful in keeping the French at bay. The northern armies were all but shattered after Doblado was defeated in an effort to retake Matehuala, and Díaz remained the most important single military obstacle to the imperialists.[25]

Maximilian and his wife Charlotte had landed at Veracruz on May 28, 1864, and proceeded by easy stages to Mexico City where they were received with enthusiasm by the monarchical elements on June 12. Though the Emperor did virtually nothing for the first five months of his reign, he demonstrated that he planned to pursue a policy of conciliation. He even made overtures to Juárez and other liberals indicating a desire to harmonize opposing factions. Juárez rejected him completely but at least one known republican, the able lawyer and scholar José F. Ramírez, entered the cabinet as a colleague of conservatives and moderate liberals alike. This quite liberal approach of Maximilian was not destined to win favor with the reactionary elements in Mexico, but the supporters of Juárez gained small comfort since the very presence of Maximilian involved a monarchy under a foreign prince.[26]

There were very few bright moments to lighten the load for Juárez during the summer and fall of 1864. Perhaps the birth of his last son at Saltillo on June 13 gave him a lift and surely there were pleasant family moments in Monterrey after the birth to his daughter of his first grandchild on July 12.[27] Such family gatherings soon ended, however, because by August 12 Juárez sent his family to Matamoros en route to the United States and safety. The French advance was consistent and the accumulation of internal problems for the Juárez administration continued.

As early as June 16, Zamacona who had never wavered in his loyalty to Juárez wrote him and expressed an almost complete loss of faith in any potential republican victory. To him, at that time, the Empire appeared well and safely established.[28] Doblado, after his decisive defeat at Matehuala, requested and received permission to leave for the United States. There he caused the government some embarrassment by trying to negotiate various matters without authority; he died, however, the following year. Many other lesser republican leaders, either feeling the situation hopeless or hoping to serve the republican cause better from outside Mexico, fled to the United States during the summer.[29]

Far more disheartening than the despair of friends was the outright traitorous activity of presumed supporters. One of the most startling defections was that of General Uraga. At the end of March he had been made commander of what was left of the army of the center though he was in fact already negotiating with the French. When his treason became known to two of his subordinates, they exposed him, and Uraga resigned and formally went over to the French, taking with him some of his officers.[30] Another traitor whose actions were to even threaten the life of Juárez was Colonel Julián Quiroga. Quiroga, who had been an ally of Vidaurri, had a few troops that would have been invaluable to the republican cause, but he insisted that he be paid for his support and that various other concessions be made to him. Juárez, in no position to refuse whatever help he could get, asked Ortega to negotiate with Quiroga. The result was that Quiroga appeared to give into Juárez's terms and was himself granted amnesty for his association with Vidaurri. Ortega again asked for cabinet changes and expressed the fear that Juárez was about to leave the country. Juárez assured the general that he intended to die in Mexico, and the matter was dropped.[31]

As the French approached Monterrey, Ortega was dispatched to Saltillo to prepare defensive measures, and by August 4 withdrawals of the government began. On August 15 Juárez departed but not before his guards were attacked in the streets of Monterrey by forces under Quiroga's command.[32] The following day Quiroga again attacked but luckily was driven off by the troops defending Juárez.[33] Before the government could reach Saltillo, the city fell to the French and Juárez's government turned off into the desert toward Durango. Until October 12 the government was literally on horseback or in carriage, but after an extremely difficult journey the entourage reached Chihuahua, which was to be home for the republican leaders for the next two years.

During the long migration a battle was fought over Durango. Ortega, with Patoni as his second in command, attacked the French at Majoma on September 21 but was defeated in a bloody engagement. This defeat was so costly to the republicans that it may well deserve to be called the last stand of their armies in the north.[34] Many persons including Juárez were critical of Ortega's handling of the campaign and Ortega felt compelled to defend himself on the grounds that his troops were simply exhausted from the long march through the desert.[35] Whatever the degree of blame Ortega should have received, the defeat left

him virtually without a command and no doubt even more dis-
enchanted with Juárez and his hopes for success than he had
been.

During the next two years the government was twice to flee
Chihuahua for Paso del Norte only to return again after the
French withdrew. Hardly stable in location, the administration
faced less internal strife than had become characteristic, and
Juárez, Lerdo, and Iglesias cemented their friendship and ex-
pended their energies to keep alive the faint republican hopes.
With some exaggeration Justo Sierra wrote that the "only hope of
the republican cause was Juárez's great soul, his stoical serenity,
his immutable faith. . . ."[36] Of course there was more to it than
that. The mere existence of a government that could provide
direction for scattered guerrilla forces, disseminate propaganda,
and function in the diplomatic arena was important.[37] All of the
activities of the government were complicated by the problems
of communications and obtaining recent news from anywhere.
After the fall of Guaymas, for example, exchanges between
Juárez and Washington went from Chihuahua or Paso del
Norte to Franklin (near El Paso), Texas, to Santa Fe then to
Kansas City and to Washington or the reverse. A letter could
take five to six weeks or more, assuming it arrived at all.[38] News
from within Mexico was even less reliable, contingent as it was
upon which locations were in whose hands at any given time
and the trustworthiness of word-of-mouth messages.

In the midst of the simple housekeeping details that must
have faced the Juárez administration after it arrived in Chihuahua, an old antagonist of the president once again stirred
up difficulty. Ortega, who had retired to Chihuahua after his
defeat at Majoma, wrote to Lerdo for an interpretation of the
constitution in regard to the end of Juárez's term.[39] The constitution simply stated that the president's term was to begin
on December 1 and last for four years.[40] Thus, Juárez might
serve until December, 1864, only three and one-half years or
until December, 1865, four and one-half years. Lerdo replied
on the same day with the assertion that the president served
until the last day of November of the fourth year following
his election.[41]

In the same exchange Ortega inquired as to his legal right to
hold the position of president of the Supreme Court, and thus

de facto vice-president, and the governorship at the same time. Lerdo very adroitly informed Ortega that he should have made a choice, as the government had informed him many times. He added that apparently Ortega preferred the governorship of Zacatecas, but under the circumstances and in view of the impossibility of providing for a successor, Juárez still considered him as the Chief Justice. Here the matter rested for the time being. During the next month, however, Ortega concluded that for his own personal safety or the benefit of the nation he could best serve by leaving Mexico and returning at some other time to engage in combat again. On December 28 he requested permission from Juárez to make such a trip.[42] Juárez approved the request and the Minister of War granted Ortega permission "as President of the Supreme Court of Justice to pass to points not occupied by the enemy" to continue defending the independence of Mexico. This permission was "for an indefinite time." With this permission, and the exact wording was to become important at a later date, Ortega left Mexico, eventually arriving in New York.[43]

Interspersed again with political blows in Juárez's life were personal losses. Shortly after his exchange with Ortega, Juárez received a letter from Romero written in mid-November telling him of the serious illness of his son Pepe in New York. Anticipating the worst, Juárez wrote to his son-in-law that he knew Romero was simply sparing him the sad news. "Really," he wrote, "my little Pepe now was no longer alive, is no longer alive, isn't that so? You know how much I suffer from this irreparable loss of my boy who was my delight, my pride, my hope."[44] Within a week his hopes had lifted, however, and he wrote to Santacilia regarding his sons' education, "I beg you," he said, "not to put them under the direction of any Jesuit, or of any sectarian of any religion; they should learn to philosophize, that is, to learn to investigate the cause or reason of things," so that they may have truth as a guide and "not the errors and prejudices that make men and peoples unhappy and degraded."[45] His hopes were doomed because within a few days he learned that his original fears had been confirmed. Probably no other personal loss comes through so clearly in the correspondence of Juárez as the loss of his son.

Bad news accumulated. Juárez must have learned of a new

military setback in Oaxaca at just about the time verification of his son's death arrived. Díaz, who had kept his forces active throughout the war, became enough of a menace to Bazaine that the latter, failing to win Díaz by other means, launched a major campaign aimed at his capture. Badly outmanned and outgunned, Díaz surrendered on February 8, once again becoming a prisoner of the French. Within seven months, after at least one failure, he engineered still another successful escape and was back in the field against the imperialists.[46] One brief piece of good military news reached Juárez in March, and he was able to congratulate Escobedo for taking Monterrey and Laredo. The improvement was brief, however, and by July the French had retaken those spots and were moving toward Chihuahua. On August 5 the government again sought refuge in Paso del Norte, and there were even rumors that Juárez planned to cross the border.

Here again personal tragedy struck. At one of the lowest points in the republican fortunes, Juárez learned in September of the death of his fifteen-month-old son Antonio.[47] Surely an end had to come to the series of misfortunes and surely Juárez had some special kind of fortitude to have endured so much. He wrote simply to his wife, "The bad luck continues; but against it what are we going to do? It is not in our hands to avoid these blows and there is only the free will to retain serenity and resignation."[48] In her letters to her husband, Margarita concealed the extreme depression she felt and, while expressing her sorrow over their loss, even found occasion to express anger at Ortega's actions.[49]

During all these months of exile from its capital, the Juárez government maintained its efforts to gain foreign support. Less important than activities in the United States were the ventures in Europe, but they were not totally neglected. Juárez had dispatched Jesús Terán to use whatever influence he could in the European capitals to bring about the withdrawal of the French. As an agent of the republican government Terán traveled back and forth across Europe with little success. He even argued the futility of Maximilian's efforts to the former private secretary of the Emperor, but the logic of his argument failed to convince Maximilian.[50]

Far more important to Juárez than decisions made by the

European nations was the attitude of the United States. Romero in Washington and Lerdo with Juárez worked diligently to gain whatever succor they might from the northern neighbor. So long as the Civil War continued in the United States they realized the limitations under which President Lincoln and Secretary Seward worked, but there were still diplomatic and physical assistance that could be given. As Juárez wrote Santacilia on April 6, 1865, he would be satisfied "if the North destroys slavery and does not recognize the Empire of Maximilian."[51] This was not quite true since Romero had already received more detailed instructions as to the kinds of aid he might solicit. Romero was to work not only to retain sympathy for Juárez and avoid the recognition of Maximilian but also work to obtain loans, military supplies, and troops. Recognizing the impossibility of day-by-day instruction, Juárez gave Romero almost complete freedom to act as he saw best except that he must not enter into any agreements that did not "preserve the integrity and independence of the national territory."[52] Even though Romero was frustrated by his inability to push Seward into a more active policy of assistance, there can be no denying that he built a residue of support for Juárez in the United States and helped maintain the active sympathy of the government. Only once did Romero seem to overstep the limits placed upon him by Juárez and that was when he became involved with Doblado in a scheme to unofficially suggest that Mexico might be willing to cede Lower California and Sonora to avoid U.S. recognition of the Empire. Fortunately, the rumor that a deal was going to be made between the United States and France was false and Seward made it clear that American sympathy for Juárez was not contingent on territorial grants. For this one lapse Romero received a stern reminder of the limits placed upon him.[53]

Though official assistance in the form of arms and men was never forthcoming, unofficial aid of both types reached Mexico while the Civil War was still going on and increased once it was over. Volunteers, both paid and unpaid, reached Mexico in small numbers. Schemes, both sincere and motivated by greed, were developed to provide arms for the republicans. Various Mexicans, including Doblado and Ortega, attempted to attract aid without authorization.[54] Once the Civil War ended, military leaders, with or without the knowledge of Washington, arranged clandestine aid, such as simply leaving ammunition dumps and other supplies at convenient places along the border where the *juaristas* could "steal" them.[55]

Perhaps more significant than any foreign assistance, and instilling in Juárez confidence that he would ultimately triumph, was his realization of the internal factors damaging to the Empire. Maximilian had turned out to be far more liberal in his policies than conservatives generally and the church in particular had anticipated. In fact, the Emperor's policy toward the church and its alienated lands differed only in detail from the Reform Laws. There was the further fact that Mexico had always had difficulty raising the funds needed for its internal development and for payments on foreign debts. The expenses of the Empire were even greater and the sources of revenue even less than before. Napoleon found his Mexican policy under attack at home and was also aware of the growing threat to France that Prussia represented. One further factor complicated the situation for Maximilian and that was the impossibility for the French army to serve two masters. Bazaine was first of all a French General and the policies he thought best were not always those of a would-be Mexican Emperor nor those of a civilian unaccustomed to the necessities of war. While all of these problems took time to build and produce the inevitable end of the Empire, Juárez considered them, while learning of Maximilian's difficulties or mistakes, and all the while kept alive the promise of eventual victory for the constitutionalist cause.

In the midst of serious matters, one comic opera incident did take place. It involved the still not forgotten Santa Anna. The aged former president had tried in February, 1864, to obtain a position of importance in the forthcoming Empire, but had been deported from Mexico by the French after he violated a promise not to issue any political pronouncements.[56] Santa Anna returned to St. Thomas a convert to republicanism. By early January, 1866, he visited with Secretary Seward who was vacationing in the Caribbean. This interview convinced Santa Anna that he would be an acceptable third alternative to Juárez and Maximilian for the United States as well as for Mexico. Such a belief made him the victim of swindlers in the United States who pretended to represent his interest. By May, Santa Anna had moved to Elizabethport, New Jersey, fully expecting the local

Mexicans to rally to his cause. Not only was that support not available, but U.S. support proved to be a mirage and Santa Anna ended up in despair with a variety of financial and legal difficulties. Even so by May, 1867, he was en route to Mexico with plans to establish a conservative republic and replace Juárez with Porfirio Díaz. He was imprisoned, tried, and ordered into exile once more, still hating Juárez and convinced that the Mexican people wanted and needed him.[57]

A far more serious threat to Juárez than Santa Anna was his military hero of the Reform, Ortega, who was fully expected to demand the presidency by the end of 1865. Juárez's correspondence during the spring and summer of 1865 indicated that he feared Ortega and his possible actions. He constantly reminded his son-in-law that Ortega had no official mission in the United States and anything he might hear to the contrary was false. He expressed disappointment that Ortega had gone to the United States instead of Sonora or Lower California. Though he admitted it was possible that the Chief Justice planned to return through the south, he felt that Ortega simply wanted to rest and would return only to claim the presidency.[58] While Juárez waited to decide what steps he should take, Ortega sought unsuccessfully the government's approval of his efforts to raise forces and matériel in the United States.[59]

On October 28, 1865, an indication of the direction Juárez intended to move appeared with the issuance by Lerdo of a circular to the governors concerning the treatment of generals, chiefs, or officials who had absented themselves from Mexico. All those who had left Mexico without authority or, with authority, and had remained away more than four months were to be imprisoned and held for trial.[60] Though Ortega had authority to remain outside the country for an indefinite time, Juárez believed this order included him, but it is doubtful that many of the state governors would have taken action against Ortega on the basis of this decree alone.

Finally, however, on November 8, Juárez took the final steps necessary to his continuance in office by issuing two decrees. The first of these decrees extended the functions of the president and the president of the Supreme Court until it was possible to hold elections.[61] The second decree declared that Ortega had voluntarily abandoned the post of president of the Supreme

Court when he remained in a foreign country without permission or commission of the government. It further stated that Ortega was to be arrested and tried on his appearance in Mexico for the crime of desertion of his post as a general of the army.[62]

The publication of these decrees brought immediate protests from some republican leaders both in and out of Mexico. Ortega issued a lengthy manifesto on December 26, 1865, from Texas detailing the events leading up to the "illegal usurpation" by Juárez. He quoted those articles of the constitution which set the length of the president's term and provided for the succession of the president of the Supreme Court in the event the office were left vacant "from any cause."[63] He further argued that under Article 95 of the constitution a magistrate might resign his office only for a grave reason and this renunciation must be approved by congress or the permanent deputation of that body. Ortega also brought up Title IV of the constitution which concerned the responsibilities of public functionaries. Under this section congress, acting as a grand jury, was to decide whether there was cause for proceeding against the president of the court when he was accused of a crime of the common order, such as the charge of desertion brought against Ortega in the second decree of November 8. The congressional decrees granting Juárez extraordinary powers specifically stated that the executive had no authority to contravene in any way the provisions of Title IV.

Ortega reviewed the various times he had held two offices and published the letter granting him permission to leave his post for an indefinite time. Although he had remained in the United States, he asserted that he had been actively engaged in aiding the republican cause and that Juárez had been fully informed of his movements. He accused the Juárez faction of plotting his removal from office and attempting to damage his military reputation prior to the expiration of Juárez's term in anticipation of the coup d'etat.[64] Among those who joined Ortega in his criticisms perhaps Prieto and Manuel Ruíz, the acting head of the Supreme Court, were the only ones of importance. Prieto's long personal friendship with Juárez, though not ended, was certainly injured in an exhaustive exchange of letters over the issue, and Ruíz had his own personal claim to the presidency to advance.

Though Juárez was apprehensive of some action by Ortega, he realized that the general lacked the necessary elements for a military move and he simply wrote to Santacilia upon receiving the protest, "I shall answer it as it should be answered, but of course a decorous answer, for it is repugnant to the dignity of a government to descend to the forbidden ground on which the silly criminal González Ortega basks."[65] Juárez expressed surprise that some Mexicans who did not desire Ortega for president still did not approve of the November decree accusing him of crimes against the state but he was, nevertheless, able to report that his government was being obeyed and respected without question by the authorities and the people.[66]

Ortega had not ended his struggle with Juárez but the course of the French intervention had shifted so that Juárez could afford to be patient and fairly complacent. Napoleon, faced with growing pressure from the United States and the failure of Mexico or Maximilian to live up to his expectations, instructed Bazaine to make one last effort to crush Juárez and then prepare to leave Mexico. Bazaine added new severity to the war by decreeing death for all who were caught fighting against the Empire, and the French armies won several small victories. Nonetheless, the *juarista* armies were growing. In February Maximilian was informed of Napoleon's decision to withdraw and immediately began to protest his need for French arms and money for a longer time. Bazaine's duty remained to withdraw from Mexico as slowly as possible in order to grant Maximilian more time to build up his native army and at the same time save face for Napoleon.[67]

In March the retreat began. Republican forces occupied Monterrey, Saltillo, and Tampico as the French withdrew. Slowly a ring of republican armies began to form and prepare for an advance on Mexico City. Maximilian still could not believe that Napoleon was serious in his decision to withdraw from Mexico. He sent a series of emissaries to Paris to attempt to convince Napoleon to reconsider, but to no avail. By July, 1866, with the French definitely committed to leave within eighteen months, Maximilian was faced with the decision of whether or not to abdicate. Characteristically, he hesitated while the Empress Charlotte set forth on an ill-fated voyage to Europe to endeavor to retain the backing of Napoleon and of the pope.

She not only failed but suffered a complete mental collapse and never returned to Mexico or saw her husband again. A native Mexican army was being built, however, with some financing by Bazaine contrary to Napoleon's wishes, and the outlook for the army was improved with the return of Miramón and Márquez from Europe ready to fight for the cause of religion and privilege once again. These slight encouragements coupled with the pressure from Mexican conservatives and other supporters of the Empire convinced Maximilian that he should make the effort to retain his throne. By this time, however, the Empire consisted of little more than Mexico, Puebla, Querétaro and Veracruz.[68]

With victory clearly on the horizon, the Juárez government ended its long sojourn in Chihuahua and moved south. Juárez, his ministers, and the state archives reached Durango on December 26 and proceeded from there to Zacatecas, where he arrived on January 22, 1867. All the news was good. Juárez had survived the worst of his trials and along with the French retreat there was a resurgence of republican armies and military leaders. News of the Austro-Prussian War meant that Napoleon would want his troops at home and there was little chance he would commit more to Maximilian.[69] Even the succession problem with Ortega appeared to have been permanently resolved in Zacatecas just a few days before Juárez's arrival. Ortega, who had spent most of the past year issuing denunciations of the government and even was rumored to have entered into negotiations with the French as an alternative to Juárez, moved to enter Mexico in October. After being delayed briefly by U.S. military authorities on the border, he and his aide, Patoni, crossed into Mexican territory on December 26. Proceeding directly to Zacatecas, Ortega pressed his claim to the presidency upon the governor there. Instead Ortega and Patoni were arrested and transferred to Saltillo. For all practical purposes the issue of Ortega's claim to the presidency was as dead as the hopes of Maximilian to rule Mexico.[70]

Meanwhile, the French promise to evacuate Mexico was rapidly being carried out with Maximilian still determined not to abdicate. General Bazaine made one last effort to force Maximilian's departure by destroying all the cannon and ammunition which he could not take with him, but when this failed to change the monarch's mind the last of the French troops marched out of Mexico City on February 5, 1867. The embarkation of the army at Veracruz began on February 14 and a month later Bazaine joined them.

The reoccupation of Mexico by republican forces was virtually uncontested until Juárez reached Zacatecas. At that point, however, took place one of those events that could have seriously altered the course of history had it turned out differently. Miramón, in a sudden and surprise attack, penetrated the city of Zacatecas and almost captured the president. Only a unique sequence of events saved the government. Though Juárez and his ministers had always traveled by coach, even when being pursued, on this one occasion they chose to flee on horseback ahead of the rifle shots of the enemy. The coaches, carrying government files, were sent along a different route. Miramón's troops, following the coaches, discovered their mistake too late to catch the fugitives. Fifteen minutes more of time or the usual procedure for flight and the course of the republic would certainly have changed.[71]

Miramón's success was short-lived. Within a few days he was driven out of Zacatecas and the republicans attacked and routed his army at San Jacinto on February 6. Juárez and his ministers moved back to Zacatecas to learn of Maximilian's order for their trial in the event of their capture, a piece of news that may well have influenced Juárez's later decision regarding Maximilian.[72] Within a few days the government moved on to San Luis Potosí to await military events. Miramón and the remnants of his army retreated to Querétaro, where Maximilian, who had taken the field as supreme commander of his army, had established the front to protect the capital. Overcoming arguments and rivalries within republican ranks, Escobedo besieged the city with up to forty thousand troops. The defending army fought valiantly and held out for almost one hundred days, from February 19 until May 15. At one point Márquez escaped from the city with plans to obtain reinforcements in Mexico City and break the siege. This too was doomed to failure. Díaz, in the south, was besieging both Veracruz and Puebla and Márquez determined that his best plan of action was to assist Puebla first. Díaz launched a brilliant attack on the city before the relief army could arrive and then surrounded the army of Márquez.

Though Márquez escaped to make one last defense of the Empire, he had done nothing to aid the besieged Maximilian at Querétaro.[73]

Rejecting an offer of personal freedom in return for the surrender of the city, Maximilian planned a dangerous and bloody attempt to break through the ring of besiegers on May 14–15. This last minute plan was foiled, however, by the treachery of one of his Mexican officers, Miguel López, who commanded the Hill of the Cross. López met with Escobedo and in return for a bribe and perhaps personal safety delivered his post to the republicans. Within a few hours the city surrendered. Maximilian was captured with his entire staff and he along with his leading generals Miramón and Mejía was held for trial by a military court.

In spite of the opposition and protests of various foreign powers the trial of the emperor and his two companions was carried out from June 11 to June 15, and the death penalty decreed. The trial was essentially for the benefit of world opinion since the government's legal right to condemn the three prisoners was clear. The comprehensive law of January 25, 1862, had provided for death to all who opposed the republic or collaborated with the French.[74] Furthermore, Maximilian, on October 3, 1865, had ordered the summary execution of captured republicans, a decree that had been carried out on several occasions. The fact that the accused would be convicted and condemned was a foregone conclusion. The only serious question concerned Juárez's decision concerning a pardon.

Exactly what influenced Juárez the most can never be known. Surely there were members of his own cabinet, especially Lerdo, who strongly urged execution.[75] At the same time there were a variety of defenders of Maximilian on purely humanitarian grounds. Interestingly, defenders of Miramón and Mejía, who actually were fighting as Mexicans for principles they believed right for their country rather than as foreign intruders, were scarce. Certainly Juárez considered the point of view that clemency was more clearly the act of a mature, civilized nation than vengeance. He must also have been moved by the personal entreaties of friends and relatives of the condemned men. Yet, though the execution was postponed for three days, Juárez decided against pardon. He insisted that public opinion required the executions but it is impossible to determine what the opinion of the Mexican people was, if there really was one on this subject. In the final analysis, Juárez's refusal to grant clemency can be seriously questioned, but it cannot be doubted that the years of fighting and the deaths of many patriotic Mexicans were directly due to the actions and pretensions of the condemned. Justice, tempered with mercy, might well have simply brought another uprising of the same reactionary elements who had caused upheavals since independence. Worse yet, a merciful act might have been interpreted as a sign of weakness and paved the way for some future foreign intervention. Perhaps the simplest explanation of Juárez's decision, in what was surely a complicated situation, is to see it as another expression of his deep concern for the carrying out of the law.

"The solemn act of justice," as Sierra called it, was carried out on the Hill of the Bells near Querétaro on June 19.[76] Two days later Mexico City capitulated to Díaz following a two-month siege. Márquez, who had defended the city, escaped to Havana, and after that there were no important defenders of the Empire or the reaction still active.

Though delayed briefly by the rains, Juárez and his government moved from San Luis Potosí toward Mexico City. Pausing briefly at Chapultepec on the request of the City Council to allow time for preparations, Juárez entered the capital on July 15 to a triumphal welcome.[77] Ten days later he was joined by his wife and children.[78] The war and the Empire had come to an end. All that had begun in 1854 had reached a new beginning. Whatever else the bloodshed of the previous decade had produced, it had given Mexico a sense of national unity that it had never before had. Furthermore, Juárez had become the symbol of that unity, of the Mexican nation. Whether he saw that with the vision of a prophet or whether he simply fell victim to a kind of megalomania and coincidentally produced the feeling, the fact remains that Juárez had brought a nation into being. Only a few weeks were needed, however, to show that living symbols have a difficult time once the crises that produced them are past.

CHAPTER VI

The Reform Continues

A NEW PHASE OF MEXICAN HISTORY BEGAN WITH THE END OF THE Empire. It had cost the nation more than 300,000 dead in battle but a nation had emerged. The Reform, the Constitution of 1857, and the government had now become one. It would take time to effect the ideals incorporated in the nation's basic document, but a beginning could be made. As Sierra has said, "the revolutionary tremors, the earthquakes that mark the period of dying volcanoes, would not be lacking: the past is not done with in a century but lingers on, gradually fading, through the course of history."[1] On the surface it would appear that Juárez was in an ideal position to overcome these obstacles. He was clearly the symbol of Mexico both to his own people and to other peoples who had gained a new respect for his nation. His party was in undisputed control of the government and Juárez's own men held most of the important federal and state offices. The Mexican people should have been and probably were tired of war and anarchy. A calm, orderly progression of government moving to solve the social and economic problems of the nation was greatly needed. Yet, Juárez was to find the path more difficult than it appeared.

"Let the people and the government respect the rights of all. Among individuals as among nations, respect for the rights of others means peace."[2] In one of his most famous statements, Juárez summed up the basic assumption upon which he felt he operated and upon which the nation's future would be secured. But who was to determine which rights had priority; what if there were differing opinions; how could one always be sure that a given president, even Juárez, was sincerely interested in the protection of rights and not the enhancement of his own power? What of the constitution, would it be carried out and with whose interpretation? How could legal and moral questions be made to mesh with the ambitions of men who wanted power and glory for themselves? Even in the difficult days of the government's hegira from Mexico City to Paso del Norte and back, conflicts had broken out in liberal ranks, sometimes over principle, sometimes over pique, and sometimes over conflicting ambitions. There was no reason to believe that these conflicts would diminish now that a real opportunity to promote oneself or a program had appeared. Surely, however, whatever contests had to be fought in Mexico could now be fought under the orderly procedures of constitutional government.

Since its adoption the Constitution of 1857 had never really been in effect except for two brief periods. The fact that Juárez delayed for a month after his return the restoration of its rule and the end of his irregular tenure in office caused an increase in suspicion as to his plans. On August 14, 1867, however, Juárez issued a *convocatoria* or a decree calling for elections for a president, congress, and members of the Supreme Court. The reason for the delay was in part apparent in that the same *convocatoria* provided for a series of reforms to be voted on by the people. Some of these proposals had the effect of amending the constitution by popular referendum while others represented fundamental changes in the law.[3] The five proposed amendments included the creation of a bicameral legislature by creating a senate, a veto power for the president that would require a two-thirds rather than a majority vote of congress to be overridden, allowing executive reports to congress to be made in writing rather than orally, restrictions on the right of the permanent deputation of congress to call special sessions of the entire body, and provisions for the presidential succession beyond the president of the court. Other issues to be voted on extended suffrage to the clergy and made the clergy and federal employees eligible to serve in congress.[4] Furthermore, the states were to vote on similar amendments to their own constitutions without following the regular amending procedures.

Opposition to the proposed changes was immediate and grew in time. The creation of a senate was seen as a dilution of the power of the congress. A two-thirds suspensive veto would make the president all-powerful since, with the right of federal employees to serve in congress, he would always have control of over one-third of that body. Written reports by ministers would deprive congressional committees of the opportunity to question these officials about matters beyond the scope of the report itself, a practice that had been used frequently and sometimes with damage in the past. All of the proposals were attacked because the set amendment procedure of the constitution, providing for a two-thirds vote by congress and ratification by a majority of the state legislatures, was ignored. Indeed, most of the opposition was devoted more to an attack upon the method chosen rather than the content of the reforms.[5] Yet, for the leaders of the reform any method that violated a constitution for which so many had fought and died was more than a mere technicality. An "electric spark" had been ignited on fertile ground.[6] All of the past fears of Juárez becoming dictatorial would be easily revived. Identification of a centralized government with conservatism was natural and the war with conservative defenders of religion was too recent for many Mexicans to accept the extension of suffrage to former enemies.[7] At least two governors, Leon Guzmán of Guanajuato and Juan N. Méndez of Puebla, felt so strongly about this matter that they refused to publish the constitutional changes and were subsequently removed from office.[8]

In the face of such surprising opposition Juárez felt compelled to issue a statement in defense of his proposals, while he left it for Lerdo to spell out specifics. Defending his chosen method by the need for speed and the ultimate sovereignty of the people, Juárez reviewed some of his reasoning. He pointed to his own experiences during some years in government and the history of other republics as justifications for changes so as to guarantee the greatness and prosperity that all wished for.[9] Though Juárez took full responsibility for the various amendments and no doubt sincerely felt a need to strengthen the powers of the president, it was his chief minister, Lerdo, who was generally felt to have been the author of the proposals and was their prime defender. Lerdo, in fact, was labeled the "Jesuit" by the opposition press because of his own seminary background and his defense of the proposal giving the clergy the vote.[10]

Lerdo was an extremely articulate and able defender of the constitutional changes and, had the issue been determined entirely on the basis of logic and need, he might have won for Juárez. In a famous circular issued on August 14, 1867, to the state governors, he spelled out some of the faults of the Constitution of 1857 and argued persuasively for a more centralized government.[11] Like Juárez he argued the need for the increased speed a popular referendum would provide over the constitutional method of amending and the sovereignty of the people as being superior to any existing law. The specific changes were discussed as necessary to provide a better equilibrium between the legislative and executive powers. They were also defended as being consistent with the federalist principles of both the Mexican nation and the United States.

Lerdo devoted his defense especially to the issue of the executive-legislative relationship. He claimed that allowing written rather than oral reports from ministers was no change in the law since the constitution said nothing about reports from ministers to congress. Since Mexico's system of government was more like the presidential system of the United States than the parliamentary systems of Europe, he felt that there was ample provision for the removal of incompetent ministers. Either the president would remove them in the face of public opinion or the legislative branch could take what amounted to impeachment proceedings. To allow members of congress to constantly vex ministers and to bring about frequent cabinet changes over private or personal matters was bad for the government. If nothing else, it had frequently led to unjustified public distrust or suspicion of the ability or program of an individual minister. As to the restriction on the powers of the permanent deputation of congress, Lerdo recalled the occasion in 1861 when as few as seven deputies called a special session of congress simply to attack the president. While he would not take away the right to call special sessions, he did feel the procedure should be made more difficult.

On the touchy subject of voting concessions for the clergy, Lerdo and Juárez both simply took the position that the clergy were citizens and should not be denied their right to vote. Anyway, the argument continued, it was better that the clergy exercise their rights directly rather than indirectly by influencing others. The procedure for extending suffrage and the right to be elected to congress were defended on the grounds that the government had such power and had exercised it in July, 1864, at Monterrey. All that was being asked was public approval.[12]

Whatever the true needs of Mexico for a stronger executive, traditional fears overcame Juárez's personal influence and the plebiscite soundly defeated the changes proposed in the *convocatoria*. At the same time, to no one's surprise, Juárez was easily reelected president. The opposition had rallied primarily behind Díaz as Juárez's major opponent. He had the advantages of a distinguished military career and the anticipated support of a large number of the some 60,000 veterans of the war against the French. Díaz also had personal cause for grievance against Juárez for having been passed over when Ignacio Mejía was named Minister of War. An astute politician, however, Díaz had taken no overt acts against Juárez and almost appears to have simply taken what support was volunteered without effort on his part. The result was an overwhelming electoral victory for Juárez; he received 7,422 votes to 2,709 for Díaz. Even Ortega was not completely forgotten in spite of his long months of imprisonment; he ran third in the election with 57 votes.[13] At the same time, Lerdo, who was Juárez's choice, was elected president of the court, although his election had to be effected by congress since no candidate had received a majority of the electoral vote.[14] Though there were election frauds and there can be no doubt that a large illiterate population was easily manipulated by the administration, it is clear that Juárez was still the popular choice of the people. But this popularity would not endure another four years.[15]

Perhaps Díaz chose more carefully his time and method for challenging the president because of the experience of the earlier contender, Ortega, whose case now surfaced again to plague Juárez. Following the announcement of Juárez's election, the opposition press led by Zamacona and *El Globo de México* announced that the time had come to expose the whole Ortega affair.[16] In early December Ortega petitioned congress for action and in the months that followed the whole history of the conflict was re-aired along with special condemnations of Juárez for the arbitrary imprisonment of the general.[17] Though a secret session of congress discussed Ortega's petition, the lack of action indicated that the government was correct in its contention that by its silence over the years congress had vindicated Juárez's decision.[18] In June, when Lerdo announced to the permanent deputation of congress that he was assuming the post as chief justice in place of Ortega, there were no public demonstrations or expressions of continued support for the Zacatecan.[19] Though the question of arbitrary imprisonment continued to be raised as an embarrassment to the government, any real danger from partisans of Ortega appeared to have disappeared.

Probably because of the lack of danger and the embarrassment his imprisonment produced, the government ordered Ortega's release along with that of Patoni on July 18, 1868.[20] They were actually freed on August 2, with Ortega moving to Saltillo and Patoni to Durango.[21] Shortly after his arrival in Durango, Patoni was killed under circumstances which cast suspicion on the Juárez administration, although subsequent investigations revealed nothing which could be construed as governmental approval of the assassination. Actually, the officer in charge of the troops responsible for Patoni's death was condemned by congress, ousted from his command, and ordered to Mexico City to stand trial. The government's actions should have proven its lack of complicity but inevitably suspicions remained.[22]

On August 19, at Saltillo, Ortega issued a statement that effectively ended his direct involvement in politics. A martyr to the last, he offered his resignation as president of the court and interim president of the republic.[23] Though rumors continued about movements against Juárez in the name of Ortega, he did nothing to inspire them; he was even defeated in an election for governor of Zacatecas since he made no effort to win the election.[24] Thus ended one of the longest continuing personal and political quarrels with which Juárez had had to deal. Even Prieto, a strong partisan of Ortega, made his peace with the president.

Political peace was still denied Juárez, however. As early as December 8, 1867, when the president spoke to the opening session of congress, he had given up the extraordinary powers granted him during the Intervention and had admitted his error in the submission of the constitutional changes in the convocatoria. Though he defended the merit of the proposals, he admitted their unpopularity and indicated that he would not even ask that the vote be counted on them. Rather, he would submit the constitutional questions to congress in the manner spelled out in the constitution itself.[25] When this was done, however, congress flatly rejected his wishes as it was to do on several other occasions during his administration. In the long run, several of the proposals were to become law but so long as they were identified with Juárez and so long as his government was an issue, they were doomed out of pure political spite if not on principle.

One source of constant irritation among Juárez's opponents was the membership of his cabinet. There had been some expectations that with the beginning of a new presidential term changes would be announced. Though the entire cabinet did submit the usual resignations, they were refused and Lerdo remained Secretary of Relations and *Gobernación* and head of the cabinet with Iglesias in Treasury, Balcárcel in *Fomento*, Mejía in War, and Martínez del Castro in Justice. Opportunities to attack the cabinet were not lacking. Since no deputy could serve in the cabinet without the prior consent of congress, Juárez was required to request such permissions for Lerdo, Balcárcel, and Iglesias immediately after congress convened in December, 1867. Congress delayed for a full month and Zamacona and other leaders of the opposition made full use of the opportunity to denounce "the Jesuit," his policies, and the Juárez administration.[26] Since the administration had a strong majority in congress the vote for Lerdo was 68–40 when it finally came, but Lerdo was forced to endure a great deal of abuse. Balcárcel escaped discussion and Iglesias resigned before congress got around to a vote on him.[27]

Iglesias's resignation, for reasons of health, brought no change of consequence. Matías Romero, who had been so long associated with Juárez, became Minister of the Treasury and Ignacio L. Vallarta became Minister of *Gobernación,* succeeding Lerdo. Lerdo still retained the more important post in the cabinet, however. It was briefly believed that the inclusion of Vallarta in the ministry indicated a broadening of the official circle and a greater concern for matters of individual guarantees that would come under his office. Within five months, however, Vallarta resigned due to disagreements with Lerdo and his belief that Juárez had lost confidence in him.[28] As Vallarta expressed it, he was resigning for "considerations of public interest and demands of personal delicacy."[29]

Meanwhile, one more attack on Juárez through Lerdo had been leveled by the Supreme Court. After assuming his position

as president of the court, Lerdo had to obtain approval to remain in the cabinet. By a seven to five vote the court refused
the dispensation.[30] Although its decision was clearly politically
motivated, there was no denying the court's legal right to act
as it had. Vallarta, prior to his resignation, had simply assumed
the additional title of Minister of Relations, with Lerdo in fact
still acting as head of the ministry. The impasse continued until
September when another request was filed by Juárez for Supreme Court permission for Lerdo to serve in the cabinet. By
then, seeing that Lerdo's influence had not diminished and no
change in policy was forthcoming, two votes shifted in favor of
Lerdo and the necessary permission was granted.[31] As Zarco
expressed the issue in *El Siglo*, "the lucid situations are better
than the shady ones, and . . . it is better to have responsible
ministers than intimate counselors."[32]

Oddly enough, at the same time that the court was attempting to control an executive perquisite, the right to name its
own ministers, it was involved in a struggle to maintain its own
independence of the legislative branch of the government. In
early 1869, the court, in effect, declared unconstitutional the
ámparo law of January 20. This law had denied *ámparo,* or
the right to appeal infringements of individual guarantees, in
judicial affairs. In reversing a lower court decision, the Supreme
Court ruled that Article 8 of the law in question was in violation of Article 101 of the constitution. Congress attempted to
order members of the court to appear before it and was itself
to sit as a grand jury. The court ruled, however, that congress
had no authority to review the court's decision and did so in
a sufficiently decorous manner as to avoid further legislative
attacks.[33] Judicial independence seemed assured for the time
being.

It was perhaps well that the court was strong under Juárez.
He had throughout his lifetime asserted a respect for the law
and, even when his opponents thought otherwise, insisted upon
observance of it. In the difficult times following the end of hostilities, and for that matter during the period of the French
retreat, there were many occasions when issues of law and
justice were uppermost in the minds of the administration.
Just as the execution of Maximilian had brought law and
justice into conflict there were many times during Juárez's post-

Intervention administration when the reconciliation of the two was difficult. If a strong, independent Supreme Court gave any encouragement to the lower courts or to the congress in the conduct of its legislative functions in this area, it was all to the good.

In January, 1862, in the face of the French attack, Juárez had issued a severe decree defining crimes against the nation and providing for the speedy trial of the accused and summary punishment of the convicted. Throughout the Intervention this law had been enforced, frequently with great severity. During the mopping-up period prior to the death of Maximilian and in the months that followed, Juárez attempted to temper this decree with a policy of severe punishment for leaders and lesser punishment or amnesty for others.[34] Such a policy inevitably led to a lack of uniformity and justice and to legitimate outrage. For these reasons there was genuine relief when Juárez abandoned his extraordinary powers in December, 1867. Unfortunately, conditions throughout the country were still unsettled. There were remnants of conservative opposition here and there. There were thousands of discharged veterans who found themselves unable or unwilling to return to productive jobs and thus were prime prospects for ambitious or disgruntled military leaders. There were also those many small bands who simply confined their activity to banditry on the highways.

The most outstanding of the true guerrilla opponents of the government were probably Miguel Negrete and Aureliano Rivera who appeared in armed opposition to Juárez shortly after Ortega's ill-fated petition to congress in 1867. Negrete had served as Minister of War during the Intervention but had gone over to Maximilian shortly before his fall. He was now faced with a desire to restore his prestige, fortune, and position but was unable to do so under a Juárez administration. Rivera apparently operated on the principle that a true liberal revolted against any authority, though there were probably somewhat more materialistic reasons in the background.[35] The actions of these two never reached the proportion of true battles and both were forced to flee Mexico within a few months, but there were other less important rebels who caused the government great discomfort.[36]

In March, 1868, conditions were unsettled to such a degree in the state of Jalisco that Juárez asked congress to reaffirm the law of January 25, 1862, to give the government the power to deal with the problem. After much debate and acrimony over the possible misuse of increased powers by the government and discussion of the government's inability to act effectively under the constitution, congress finally acted.[37] Faced with disorder not only in Jalisco but in Sonora, Sinaloa, Yucatán, Puebla, and Guerrero, congress felt obliged to provide some means of dealing with the widespread problem of banditry, assassination, and general upheaval. Though the government was forced to make some concessions, including the suspension of individual guarantees only until December 31, 1868, a law was passed on May 8 granting emergency powers.[38] Within a month the government had obtained another law, which suspended individual guarantees for one year for kidnapers and bandits.[39]

Throughout the legislative debates over powers to handle rebellion, Juárez's opposition was inclined to favor more extensive amnesty than he did. In addition, men like Zarco argued that the government was willing to extend amnesty to those Mexicans who had sided with the French but unwilling to grant similar relief to Mexicans whose only crime was a desire to defend the constitution against the usurpations of Juárez. No bill could be passed until October, 1869, and it was clearly a defeat for the administration in that it extended broad exemptions to all who had been guilty of treason, sedition, conspiracy, and other crimes against the public order prior to September 19, 1867.[40] Fortunately, by the time the law was enacted, the more serious revolts against the government had been ended.

Though there were disturbances throughout 1869 and 1870, some almost chronic, the culmination came in January, 1870, with an organized movement led by Governor Trinidad García de la Cadena of Zacatecas. Having earlier refused to join a revolt started in San Luis Potosí, García, on January 8, issued a plan calling for the overthrow of Juárez and the recognition of Ortega as president.[41] Certainly involved in García's decision and the support he received were the unparalleled cruelties committed by government officers the previous year as well as his own personal ambitions.[42] Ortega removed himself as an issue on January 22, one month before the revolution was crushed by Sóstenes Rocha and Escobedo, by issuing a statement

asserting that he had never been consulted concerning the revolt and the insurgents had no reason to involve him.[43] By the
end of March the rebels were scattered and inconsequential.
Other minor revolts flared up during the remainder of the year
but nothing large enough to threaten the government.

One of the reasons the Juárez administration was able to
handle rebellion as well as it did, and oddly enough one of the
causes of some rebellious activity, was the fact that the army
had been reorganized into a strong, small entity. Clearly, over
60,000 men were not needed once the fighting had ended and
maintaining that large an army was expensive. Thus in July,
1867, the army was reduced to around 18,000 men and still took
up much too large a percentage of the national budget.[44] This
smaller army under the overall direction of Mejía was divided
into five commands under Generals Régules, Díaz, Escobedo,
Corona, and Álvarez. Díaz's relationship with Juárez by this
time was cool and he considered leaving the army but was convinced by Juárez to remain for a time; he later retained his
command for his own personal political reasons. In retrospect,
it is easy to see that reducing the size of the army so rapidly without prior planning was a mistake.[45] This was true because so
many of the common soldiers joined the marauders on the highways and the occasional rebellions. There were also victorious
generals who wanted privilege and power for themselves and
their friends. The army organized under Mejía, while it never
eliminated all threats, was at least able to restore a semblance
of order by the end of 1870. Juárez disarmed some of the generals with flattery and when that failed, promoted their subordinates as foils. All the while Juárez's own prestige was sufficient to offset the appeal most military men would have had
to the public.[46]

Whatever Juárez's successes, and the mere survival of his
administration was not the least of these, he had committed
errors and there was much that was still undone. Some felt they
saw fatigue in the president and that he devoted himself to
simple matters of routine. The defeat of the *convocatoria* must
have taken away some of his confidence. Keeping Lerdo in the
cabinet provided the opposition with a good bit of ammunition
whatever the minister's value to the president. Juárez's inability
to handle rebels under existing law could lead one to believe

that he wished more punitive legislation to use against political opponents. The arbitrary imprisonment of Ortega simply could not be justified and Juárez was fortunate that the general had not lent his name to armed rebellion. The traditional intervention by the government in elections, however customary, was not in line with the ideals of constitutional, republican government. The severity and bloodshed with which rebels were crushed and punished must have seemed to illiterate and ignorant peasants little different from the actions of a Miramón or a Santa Anna.

Yet it is wrong to assume that Juárez was personally responsible for all that did not go well. The congress had done little or nothing to advance the nation economically, socially, or politically. Reforms of any kind were virtually impossible to obtain. Economic reconstruction was a matter of time as well as of policy. Similarly, the restoration of normal relations with other nations would require time and only then could foreign economic policies be developed for the benefit of Mexico. Internal peace, security, and order were being sought but until reasonable safety existed inside Mexico foreign investment and foreigners would remain scarce. If Mexico had had good economic prospects in the short term, if there had been adequate foreign and internal trade, perhaps potential leaders would have benefited themselves and the nation in the economic area. As it was, until that day came, politics and military-political activity remained the easiest way to power and the incumbent president was the antagonist.[47] Politics remained reduced to personal attacks more than debates over alternative programs, and the nation was the loser.

There was some hope that the congressional elections of 1869 would clear the air a bit and provide more certain direction for a liberal program. Unfortunately, this did not take place. The opposition, organized as the Constitutional Liberal Party, simply raised the old issues against the *juaristas*. The *convocatoria* was cited as evidence of the government's lack of regard for the constitution. The need for economic development was proclaimed along with economy and efficiency in government. The independence of the states from federal control was asserted and the usual charges of government use of bribes, threats, and force in the election were leveled. The result of the election was a strongly pro-government congress. After all, the charges of rigging elections were true, but in all fairness the opposition did the same thing wherever it could. There simply were not many opportunities for the outs. Public apathy and indirect voting procedures always lend themselves to manipulation by an incumbent administration.[48] More important than the failure of opposition candidates to win control of congress was the growing division within government ranks into *juaristas* and *lerdistas*. The exact result of this factionalism was not yet clear but it could hardly be expected to help Juárez in his dealings with congress.[49]

One thing was clear to *juaristas, lerdistas,* and the opposition and that was the great need for the financing of programs of social and economic development. Simply because the government had managed to operate for so many years with little or no resources, did not change this fact. In one sense Juárez had the best opportunity any president of the republic had ever had to raise revenue. Virtually all revenue now came to the government since it took the position that intervention by a foreign nation or recognition of the Empire invalidated all earlier treaties. Thus monies previously earmarked for payment of a variety of European debts were theoretically released for other uses by the government. In addition, the trauma of the past decade of warfare had made Mexico a more unified nation than it had ever been, especially since there was a faint possibility that localism and the resultant local control over financial resources could be reduced. Surely, the restoration of peace would also see a resumption of something approaching normal commercial and agricultural activity and allow the extractive industries, serving as the basis for the Mexican economy, to revive.

All of this was true but the debit side of the ledger was much longer. The cost of reconstruction of a war-torn nation was inevitably high. National wealth had been lost for over eleven years and could never be regained. For the moment, commerce and agriculture were virtually paralyzed and there was no native industry worthy of the name. There was not enough economic activity to provide for needed jobs let alone the financial requirements of the nation. The reconstruction of the economy would have to begin without foreign credit or substantial foreign investment. No national of another country was likely to risk his life or his person in a nation having no diplomatic connections with his own. There was not a great deal of domestic capital to turn to either. Many of the wealthy Mexicans who had supported the Empire had left the country or had sent their wealth overseas. Others represented the uneasy rich who were afraid to invest in such uncertain times and were a part of the high society in the large cities that feared and opposed Juárez throughout his tenure in office.[50] Until the threat of banditry and rebellion was reduced, few, either Mexican or foreign, would be willing to risk their capital in Mexico. Removal of this problem was, at the same time, a concern and an additional expense for the government. Quite apart from the question of private capital, the government found it difficult to establish a sound basis of taxation. There were inadequate statistics upon which to base a program, and a recalcitrant congress influenced by tradition was slow to act. Nationalism had not done as much as hoped in removing the old problem of local autonomy versus the federal government. As one writer put it, the state leaders "do not know how to command and do not want to obey."[51]

In the face of such horrendous financial problems Juárez was ill prepared to deal with the situation. While he had had personal experience as governor of a state and knew enough to realize the need for revenues, he could be forgiven for lacking a sophisticated understanding of the needs of a developing, or in fact at this time underdeveloped, nation. The primary responsibility for advancing an economic program fell to Romero, the Secretary of the Treasury, although it is doubtful that Romero made any substantial proposals without the knowledge and agreement of Juárez. It is impossible to fault Romero for his efforts. He worked as diligently as any member of the administration and understood a great deal of what needed to be done. Basically, he proposed to concentrate and systematize the revenue gathering of the nation, to readjust continually the tariff schedules, to transfer the government's dependence upon external income to internal sources and to keep good account of income and expenditures while eliminating fraud and mismanagement. These were hardly easy goals to obtain, especially since regional interests had also to be taken into account and sectional prosperity was as much demanded as national.

Romero presented his major set of proposals to congress in

April, 1869, with additional executive actions and proposals as required.[52] One of his first goals was an increase in customs duties since over one-half of the federal revenue came from that source. The issue was simple; more trade meant more income. Obviously, the government's continual action to reduce danger on the highways was aimed partly at this goal. In addition, however, there was need for a program of internal improvements: roads, railroads, and communications facilities.[53] The outstanding effort in this direction was the completion of the Mexico to Veracruz railroad, a project whose history dated back to 1857. In 1868 the government began renegotiation of a contract with the British company that had started construction. The new contract required the approval of congress and was immediately opposed and revised by the opposition led by Zamacona. By a concerted effort the administration was able to defeat the revision and sign the proposed contract.[54] Grants were also issued for the construction of two other railroads, one from the capital to Túxpan and the other across the Isthmus of Tehuantepec. Other smaller construction projects were initiated, including a variety of new roads and the extension of telegraph facilities.[55] Clearly these construction projects would all require time to produce benefits and other programs were needed in the meanwhile.

Romero realized that a reduction in existing tariffs could actually produce an increase in income on the assumption that more goods would be imported. For this reason he proposed as one of his major plans a complete revision of the tariff laws and an overall reduction if not removal of existing tariffs. Such a change was badly needed. The tariffs were in most instances too high; there were too many and they changed too frequently. Although the government and congressional committees worked diligently on a set of changes, it was impossible to obtain congressional approval. Tariffs were an old and consistent source of revenue as well as a complicated one. Congress was simply too critical and too unwilling to upset tradition to make the changes Romero felt were needed. Not only was the national tariff schedule a problem but the continued existence of the *alcabala,* or state customs duties, was a deterrent to increased commerce. These interstate duties were unconstitutional but were still in force. Romero tried unsuccessfully to eliminate this

tax by diplomacy and even bribery, that is, by relieving any
state that abolished the tax of certain payments it had to make
to the federal government.[56]

Most important of all to Romero were changes in the law
designed to revive mining. He, like the rest of the administration, felt that Mexico's economic development lay in the extractive industries. At the time direct taxes on mining amounted to
almost twenty-five percent of gross income, a figure much too
high in Romero's view. He proposed that this be changed so
that mines would be subject to only one five percent tax on
profits. Further, he asked congress to remove all taxes on the
export of gold and silver bullion and levy a one percent tax on
the export of minted gold and eight percent on minted silver.
All other mineral products were to be exported free of any
tax. Here again congress refused to act and chose to stay with
what had been a traditional source of revenue. In this case
there were grounds for arguing that programs aimed at increasing the export of money from Mexico were detrimental
and that what was needed were more and varied industries.
Still, Mexico was in no position at the time to become involved
in serious debates over total economic development when a start
in all areas was required.

Other proposals by Romero were rejected by congress. One
would simply have raised revenue by taxing inheritances on
the basis of relationship rather than amount. Another would
have taxed uncultivated lands held by large landowners. Romero hoped this would not only provide revenue but would
encourage use of such lands or their sale thus providing some
social as well as economic reform. One of the most discussed
proposals of Romero was not strictly speaking a revenue measure
but a currency reform. He wanted to issue 18,000,000 pesos in
treasury notes to offset the seasonal nature of the government's
revenue from customs. By issuing enough notes at the beginning
of a year to meet anticipated expenses, the government would
be able to pay its obligations regularly, something it had not
been able to do in the past at some expense in interest charges.
These treasury notes would also provide a much needed me-
dium of exchange since each year twenty-one to twenty-three
million of the twenty-four million pesos minted were exported.[57]

Romero's inability to obtain more of his desired legislation complicated a miserable bureaucratic situation. In February, 1868, he reported that the books were so disorganized that he could not even figure the government's income for the fiscal year.[58] Thus as the end of Juárez's term approached, he could point to few significant gains that he had been able to achieve in the economic sphere. While he had a majority in congress, it was an unruly one and Juárez's prestige, Romero's efforts, and Lerdo's talents were insufficient to bring it into line on very many substantial pieces of legislation.

One of the obstacles to increased foreign commerce and investment was the foreign policy Juárez adopted at the close of the Intervention. While Mexico was anxious and willing to resume normal relations with those European countries that had supported or recognized Maximilian, national pride dictated that the European nations had to make the first move.[59] The result was a semi-isolationist foreign policy directed by Lerdo, a policy that reflected a strong national inferiority complex and touchiness in the face of presumed insults by others. For example, a representative of the Austrian government arrived in Mexico with instructions to return Maximilian's body to Europe. Although the visit was really of a private nature, Lerdo insisted that proper written requests be made by appropriate Austrian authorities. As soon as these were forthcoming, the Mexican government gladly cooperated.[60] Lerdo's cool treatment of the British consul was sufficient to cause his recall at the very time that Romero was searching for ways to increase foreign investment and trade. Whether the Juárez administration could have retained its self-respect and the respect of other governments with a more conciliatory policy is difficult to say. If other aspects of the investment climate in Mexico had been completely favorable, it is doubtful that the foreign policy attitude alone would have made a great deal of difference.

Relations with the United States certainly did not suffer from the stigma of support for Maximilian, and Juárez made it clear that he would welcome American capital. Nevertheless, American investors were hesitant about risking their funds in Mexico. Diplomatic relations between the two governments remained friendly, however. A Mixed Claims Commission was established to settle questions arising from private claims since the Treaty of Guadalupe Hidalgo, and other expressions of good will were exchanged.[61] One of the more noteworthy examples was a visit by former Secretary of State Seward to Mexico during which he expressed extremely high praise of Juárez. Since Seward had been earlier identified with American expansionist designs, his visit did much to reduce fears on the part of Mexico and signified a new era of friendship between the two nations.[62] Again, however, such friendly exchanges did nothing to improve the economic picture in Mexico.

By 1871, relations had been reestablished with the German Confederation, Italy, and Spain, and time and necessity would heal the wounds Mexico felt.[63] Time and circumstances helped Juárez in other ways. The defeat of Napoleon at Sedan must have been noted with pleasure and Juárez expressed his hopes for a free and peaceful government for the French people. Equally interesting was news of the defeat of Marshal Bazaine, who had caused so much grief for Mexico, at Metz and his later conviction of treason. Juárez does not appear to have been a particularly vengeful type but he was human and it is hard to believe he felt no joy in the misfortunes of his former enemies.

It is well that he had some things for which to rejoice because personal misfortune continued to plague him. In October, 1870, when he was sixty-four years old, he suffered a stroke of some kind that caused brief concern for his life. Fortunately it was not serious. The following January, however, his wife died from a long and painful illness at the age of forty-four. How seriously Juárez felt this loss can only be surmised from the private secular funeral that he held. While he and his wife had been separated for much of their married life, they had had twelve children, suffered the loss of five of them, and shared by correspondence at least much of the trial and tribulation each had felt during their separations. The nation mourned the loss of Señora Juárez as much in honor of her husband as for her own contribution to the cause he had come to represent. There was even a brief political truce in recognition of Juárez's personal grief but it was not to last. Indicative of this was the fact that Rivera and Negrete, whom Juárez had pardoned, acted as pallbearers. One of them even soldered the coffin, a skill he had once practiced.[64]

No account of Juárez's administration can be complete without emphasizing his efforts in the field of education. His own racial origins plus the convictions he acquired with experience created in Juárez almost a feeling of duty to remove the superstition, ignorance, and related alcoholism of the Indians. He had faith that education would provide much of the solution to the problems of his people and would also serve as a foundation for a stronger national economy. Related to his belief in education was the further conviction that it should be secular so as to combat some of the unfortunate effects of Catholicism. Though Juárez considered himself a Catholic, he realized some of the virtues of Protestantism for Mexico. On one occasion he remarked to Justo Sierra that he "would like to see the Indians converted to protestantism; they need a religion that will teach them to read and not to waste their pennies on candles for the saints."[65]

In this effort to separate education and religion Juárez's Minister of Justice and Public Instruction, Antonio Martínez de Castro, in 1867 appointed a committee to reorganize public education. The ultimate leader of the committee and the man most responsible for the philosophy that directed their efforts was Gabino Barreda. Barreda had obtained a medical degree in France and while there had been tremendously influenced by the positivist philosophy of Auguste Comte. Thus Barreda, like Comte, believed that education could and should be based on science and humanitarianism. Positivism became almost a substitute for the negative influence of religion. By the application of science proper values and beliefs would be determined and then state-controlled education would produce uniformity in thinking. This uniformity in turn would produce order, the base upon which progress could be obtained.[66] Like Comte, Barreda believed that the human mind had passed through three successive states: religious, metaphysical, and positive. Clearly Mexico had passed through a religious stage. To Barreda the reform was the metaphysical stage and the emerging liberalism was to be the positive stage. While Barreda and his followers claimed that they believed in the liberal concept of freedom as the proper climate for obtaining the desired order and progress, they soon dropped the emphasis on freedom. As dissent developed, it became apparent to Barreda that toleration of liberty of thought was a detriment to the desired results. In time, then, positivism would become a force supporting a far more authoritarian state than Juárez envisioned.

For the time being, however, the most obvious result of the committee's efforts was a plan for education in the Federal District adopted into law on December 2, 1867.[67] This plan spelled out a curriculum that was supposed to prepare Mexicans for the world in which they lived. It emphasized practical courses such as reading, arithmetic, and science with some attention paid to government, history, and geography. Hopefully, primary education was to be available to all, even the poor, and thus could become compulsory. This program was too limited to indicate much of what might happen. There simply was not enough money during Juárez's administration to develop a total national program, and even as the program grew, it would be some time before it could bear fruit. While the entire educational system can be criticized for its inadequacies, and positivism drew some just and honest criticism as a basic philosophy, it remains clear that Juárez realized the importance of education for his country. Time would demonstrate even more clearly the massive difficulties in the way of an adequate system, but Juárez cannot be faulted for trying to begin.

As the last year of Juárez's presidential term began, he could look back on a set of extremely mixed results. The army had been greatly reduced and what remained had been made efficient, but there were still constant military threats to peace and order. Economic progress had been made, but nothing approaching the rate needed or indeed anticipated had been achieved. Social progress was seriously lacking. Nothing of consequence had been done to touch the age-old question of a need for land reform. Foreign relations remained largely undecided and desirable foreign investment was unobtainable. Republicanism had been preserved but the trend toward centralism was unmistakable and feared. Democracy had not yet replaced controlled elections, and personalism was as much of a plague to politics as it had been in the days of Santa Anna. The power of the church had been limited and secular education received official support but the fruits of these changes were still in the future. Freedom of speech and of the press did exist and were used constantly by the opposition to remind the public of Juárez's limitations. The man who had become the symbol of the nation had been reelected in 1861 largely because the times required it. He had been elected still again in 1867 as a reward for his services and as a rebuff to those who had been attacking the nation in the preceding years. By 1871, however, there was reason to doubt that Juárez was needed any longer. A new generation had come of age with new ideas and perhaps new vigor and vitality. The spirit of the constitution prohibited reelection no matter what had been done at the two previous presidential elections. Juárez could have retired into a well-deserved place of honor among his own people and the world, leaving the continuing problems of restoration to others. This he chose not to do.

Exactly how and when Juárez determined to seek another term can never be known. He kept his own counsel and revealed to no one exactly what influenced his decision. Perhaps he feared either of his most likely successors, Díaz and Lerdo. Perhaps he needed the life of politics to compensate for the loss of his wife and therefore his lack of a private life to which to retire. It may be that one historian's assessment of all three of the major political figures of the time says all there was to say: "Juárez believed he was indispensable; while Lerdo regarded himself as infallible and Díaz as inevitable."[68] Certainly Juárez had been forced to close his eyes and ears to opposition so often in the past for what had been just reasons and it would not be unusual if he saw the opposition of 1867–1871 in the same light. There had always been a stubborn streak in the man and his stoical attitude in the face of adversity would ever influence his actions. He also may have been influenced by what he hoped to do for the Mexican people, and he may have felt that other leaders might take other directions. He even had every reason to think that the public owed him another term in office.

The debate can only continue. Juárez can be criticized for deciding to remain in office but his reasons cannot be criticized so long as they are unknown. In any event, by January, 1871, there was no doubt that Juárez was a candidate for reelection, and the political campaign that had actually started four years earlier was underway. Before it was over much of Juárez's glory had become tarnished and his life's final chapter had become almost an unfortunate aftermath to a noble and distinguished career.

CHAPTER VII

Election of 1871 and After

IN JANUARY, 1871, LERDO RESIGNED FROM THE CABINET.[1] THIS WAS not the first time he had offered to resign. As early as July, 1870, and again in September he had tried.[2] The actual separation had not occurred, however, until a special situation had arisen and had forced it. The specific issue involved was the disputed election of an *ayuntamiento* or city council for Mexico City in December, 1870. Since this body supervised local elections, it was important who controlled it or whom it favored. The supporters of Lerdo had won control of the council but the *juaristas* argued that the election was fraudulent and elected their own council. Unable to effectively resolve the issue, the cabinet decided that the existing council should simply continue in office until congress acted.[3]

The way in which Juárez had handled this problem indicated clearly that he intended to be a candidate for reelection. Although Lerdo had yet to make it clear that he was a presidential candidate, astute observers knew that he was. For him to remain in the cabinet would have been even more difficult than it had been, thus his resignation.[4] Zamacona, as head of the supporters of Díaz, may have helped to push this resignation and thus unite the opposition to Juárez, but in any event Lerdo's resignation represented an unfortunate end to seven years of intimate relationship between the president and his minister.[5] Lerdo, either because of personal ambition or honest disagreement with Juárez, had become the leader of an opposition party in congress and, though he had been an active and effective supporter of Juárez over the years, he had come to disagree with Juárez both on personal and ideological issues. For one thing, Lerdo believed that an attempt by Juárez to continue himself in office would produce an armed revolt by the *porfiristas*. He had even urged Juárez's resignation as a means of avoiding such a revolt. Juárez, as had been the case in similar past disagreements, argued that "he was not resigning, because the law and his duty prohibited. . . ."[6] Because of the open disagreement between the two men that had emerged there was nothing Juárez could do but accept Lerdo's resignation with little more than polite thanks for his service to the government.[7] By this time Juárez "saw Lerdo transformed from an intimate friend into just another traitor with ambitions."[8]

Actually, of course, Lerdo was hardly a traitor, but he was an ambitious man. He had every reason to assume that Juárez would step down from the presidency and support his own claim to the office, and it had to be a major disappointment when he found this was not to be the case. Lerdo's supporters in congress had been a major faction for at least the last two years and, though they were supposedly pro-administration, they had become almost as much of an opposition party as the older opposition elements had been. Some members of the administration, especially Secretary of War Mejía, had felt that Lerdo should stay in the government and avoid the kind of split in the administration that might provide encouragement to those opponents of Juárez who were willing to resort to more than political opposition. In addition, he had high regard for Lerdo's contributions to the government during the last years, while others felt that Lerdo was the evil influence that had been operating on Juárez for the past seven years.[9]

Still and all, Lerdo did have designs on the presidency and there were a number of Mexicans who supported his ambitions. Men of property, most of the more socially prominent people, lawyers and writers, as well as some of the bureaucracy could be counted among the *lerdistas*.[10] The two most influential leaders of the *lerdista* faction were Ramón Guzmán and Manuel Romero Rubio. Guzmán was Lerdo's chief agent in congress and Rubio was a lawyer often useful for his diplomatic ability.[11] A significant portion of the press was either pro-Lerdo or anti-Juárez, *El Siglo* being the major newspaper espousing Lerdo's cause.[12] Even Iglesias, as old a compatriot of Juárez as Lerdo, resigned from the cabinet at the same time and was considered a partisan of his fellow cabinet member.[13] Still other prominent Mexicans, such as Isidro Montiel y Duarte, an academician, and Hilarión Frías y Soto, a prime member of the intelligentsia, were *lerdistas*.

One could add such famous historians as Julio Zárate and José María Vigil to their ranks.[14]

Perhaps more important than the caliber of Lerdo's supporters was the support he had been able to establish prior to his resignation among state governors and local administrators, men who would have some control over the forthcoming elections. While head of the cabinet he had been able to secure the appointments or the friendships of governors in San Luis Potosí, Puebla, Michoacán, Jalisco, Hidalgo, Guanajuato, and Morelos.[15] This support would probably have been enough even without the council of Mexico City to give Lerdo an election victory, but after his resignation Juárez changed enough of the governors to turn the results around.

Insofar as program was concerned, the *lerdistas* presented little that was new. They supported the policies for which Lerdo had been responsible as a cabinet member and promised to carry out the liberal ideas of the Reform. The party promised a continuation of the dignified foreign policy of the past, an expansion of educational opportunities, enforcement of the laws, respect for the sovereignty of the states and support of individual rights. They promised in somewhat vague terms to develop the economy on the basis of free enterprise and to free the government of corruption and waste.[16] One thing supporters of Lerdo tried to make clear was that they had no personal animosity toward Juárez but were opposed to his second reelection. Furthermore they offered no support to any talk of revolt against Juárez whatever the results of the election.[17]

Less of a threat to Juárez in terms of control over key offices and officials but more of a threat in terms of popular support was young General Díaz. Díaz had been the only major opponent of Juárez for the presidency in 1867 and had remained the choice of most of the old opponents of the Juárez-Lerdo administration. These *porfiristas* also included a number of discontented military men, some idealistic young liberals, and the accumulated enemies of Juárez.[18] Díaz had retired from the army to his ranch at La Noria near Oaxaca and appeared to disassociate himself from much of the activity in his name. In Mexico City, however, Justo Benítez directed a *porfirista* campaign with the able support of Zamacona and others. In the state of Oaxaca Félix Díaz, the candidate's brother, was governor and provided a safe and important base for the party's operations. The party was not well organized in most states but rather counted on laws guaranteeing free elections and Díaz's personal popularity as their path to victory.

The *porfirista* program was less important than the candidate and differed little from the *lerdistas*. *El Mensajero,* the major newspaper supporting Díaz, printed its program on January 11, 1871. Again defense of state and individual rights was promised along with a government free of corruption and waste. Naturally, free elections were emphasized as well as defense of the Constitution of 1857.[19] For the most part the *porfirista* press was content with extolling the virtues of their candidate, his military exploits, and the errors of the Juárez-Lerdo administration. The *convocatoria* was recalled, the inability of the government to maintain order without excessive powers was emphasized, and the need for new men from the new generation was pointed out. Actually, though Díaz avoided association with any of the revolutionary or pseudo-revolutionary movements that troubled Juárez, his failure to issue some statement, like Ortega's, disassociating his name made him at least morally responsible. The fact was, then, that the *porfiristas* were to a large extent responsible for the very troubles they blamed Juárez for inability to deal with.[20]

The *juaristas* were of course forced to stand on the record of the administration and used *Diario Oficial* and other newspapers to remind the people of past accomplishments and future hopes. Most of the bureaucracy and the federal army could be counted in the president's camp and, as usual in national elections, were expected to be decisive in determining the result.

Because *lerdistas* and *porfiristas* alike realized the traditional pattern of fraud in elections and government interference, it is in some ways strange that they went through so much of the process that might be anticipated in a free election. Yet, without the motions, they would have been in no position to charge Juárez later with a rigged election. At any rate, there was at least a small chance that they could defeat him. Thus, political clubs sprang up all over the country in support of the various candidates and most newspapers became little more than propaganda vehicles for the contenders. Though truly national political organizations did not exist, the beginnings of what might have been true political parties emerged. To Juárez's credit, the election campaign during the first six months of 1871 was virtually free. Freedom of the press was allowed and political activity was generally not interfered with. Knowing that he had the monies and machinery of the government behind him as well as the army's power wherever needed, Juárez could well afford to be generous. Yet, he had been the victim of so much abuse during the difficult years of civil war and intervention, that the freedom to continue attacking the president would inevitably impugn any future administration. Juárez would have been only human had he chosen to deny some freedom of criticism simply to maintain respect for the government. At the same time, Juárez recognized Díaz's contributions to the nation whatever his limitations may have appeared to be as a potential president. To silence spokesmen for a military hero, whom some already believed to have been deprived of his just rewards, would have been dangerous. As far as Lerdo was concerned, Juárez had been too close to him and had relied upon him too heavily for the past seven years to turn against him completely. Indeed, the relationship between these two contenders after Lerdo left the cabinet remained a true mystery.[21]

The only possible way for the opposition to defeat Juárez was to work together. The result was a strange and impractical coalition of *lerdistas* and *porfiristas* in congress. Though leaders of both factions insisted that no agreement, tacit or otherwise, existed, the *juarista* press continually referred to one and could produce consistent evidence of voting patterns that indicated its existence.[22] The first such example had been the *lerdista* victory in the city council of Mexico City, a victory that had been possible only with *porfirista* support. After the cabinet had been unable to resolve the city election between the contending factions, a congressional committee had been appointed to study the question. The committee recommended that the *lerdista* council be installed. Even so, *juaristas* argued that such interference in domestic affairs was unconstitutional. When the vote was taken in congress the coalition of Juárez's opponents won a narrow victory. Juárez then declared that congress would have to pass a law before he would act, and even after another vote by congress, he refused to seat the *lerdista* council. The *lerdistas* attempted to assume their posts anyway and were expelled by the governor of the Federal District. Congress, appalled at this action against its decree, ordered Juárez to seat the pro-Lerdo group. Juárez, faced with a truly dangerous situation, gave in for the moment but made it clear that he still objected. Apparently, the *lerdistas* had won a victory.[23]

The struggle over the *ayuntamiento* was a crucial part of *lerdista* strategy. Their only chance for victory required that governors or other officials having control over elections and supporting Lerdo remain in power. Their estimates showed that Lerdo had enough support to keep any candidate from receiving the necessary majority of the vote. Consequently, the election would fall to congress where every state delegation had one vote. The *lerdistas* planned to change the procedure so that the vote would be on a one man-one vote basis instead. Reasonable estimates indicated that Lerdo would probably be elected president under such a system.[24] Without *porfirista* support this strategy had no chance and, even with the coalition working together, there were significant obstacles. For another thing, the emphasis on the independence of the states was so contrary to Lerdo's own centralistic philosophy of government, it must have seemed all too obvious what he was attempting to do.

The *porfiristas* had to take a calculated risk. Unless they supported some of the Lerdo proposals they could not get reciprocal support for changes in the law that they needed. Believing that Díaz was the popular candidate of the people, they believed their prime requirement was a free election. Thus they wished to repeal the law allowing the president to declare a state of siege under which control of elections by the military was easy and they also wished to limit the budget items which Juárez might be able to use in influencing the outcome of the election. The Díaz supporters were convinced that by working with other Juárez opponents to keep him from winning a majority of the votes, they would be able to demonstrate their candidate's overwhelming public support and the *lerdistas* would finally help elect Díaz. This complicated strategy required working with *lerdistas* and at the same time creating more ill-will between *lerdistas* and *juaristas*.[25]

When congress opened a special session in March, 1871, it was obvious immediately that Juárez was in for a battle. Zamacona, one of his leading opponents, was elected president of the congress and used his post to denounce the president. Other members of the assembly were more open in their denunciation of Juárez than was usually the case in such a legislative assembly, and *juarista* delegates were equally strong in their counter-attacks. This state of affairs continued into the regular session of congress that began in April.

The first major piece of legislation passed by the anti-Juárez coalition on May 8 came after lengthy debate but represented something for both *lerdistas* and *porfiristas*. This was a law that prevented military personnel from leaving their barracks on election day and required that they vote at their base. The restriction applied to both state and federal elections and also prevented the president from calling out the armed forces during the months preceding an election. At the same time, the system of voting in congress was changed from one vote for each state to one vote for each individual.[26] Thus the *porfiristas* hoped to obtain the freer elections they sought and the *lerdistas* the preferred method of congressional balloting.

Since this law in one sense was discriminatory toward the military, top army men publicly denounced it and were even more unanimous in their support of Juárez than they might already have been. The administration, in promulgating the law, expressed its disapproval and made clear that it had little intention of seriously enforcing it.[27] Juárez must have had some qualms about the position in which he found himself since he had always been such an outspoken advocate of the law's being observed. Yet, here again, as had been the case on previous occasions, he was somehow able to rationalize which laws needed to be observed and which could be ignored though not broken.

The congressional opposition was still not through. On May 24 a law was passed that declared unconstitutional an existing law allowing the president to proclaim a state of siege if he thought it necessary when congress was not in session. The *juaristas* fought this measure as they had other acts of the opposition even though the new law would not prevent the president from declaring a state of siege once congress adjourned.[28] It appeared that the alliance of *lerdistas* and *porfiristas* was doing well, but they had hardly won all they sought. The hopes of limiting the budget failed and efforts to embarrass the administration by investigations of top officials also led nowhere. All the while Juárez's supporters were building up his reservoir of support and doing their best to destroy the uneasy alliance that made up the opposition.[29]

In the state of Jalisco, for example, Juárez acted, after Lerdo's resignation from the cabinet, to remove the pro-Lerdo governor. Further, the *juarista*-controlled legislature of the state removed all town councils and proceeded to hold new elections that guaranteed pro-Juárez administrations and thus a pro-Juárez presidential vote.[30] Similarly, *juaristas* strengthened their control in San Luis Potosí and Puebla. The issue of control of the city council of Mexico City had to be postponed until after congress adjourned. Once that had occurred on May 31, the *juarista* governor of the Federal District, Gabino Bustamante, ordered the *ayuntamiento* suspended on the grounds that he had evidence they planned fraudulent elections. For the moment, the old city council elected in 1869 was to take over.[31] Though the permanent deputation of congress violently opposed this action, Juárez announced that he had investigated the matter and determined that the governor had acted legally and the national government had no cause to interfere.[32]

Complete destruction of the opposition's voting alliance could not be achieved but it could certainly be splintered. The administration was not unwilling to use bribery to win an occasional weak opponent over and certainly flattery or promises of rewards sometimes worked.[33] Zamacona became convinced that, for some reason, Benítez was no longer working with the *lerdistas* and was even sometimes working with the *juaristas*. When he was unable to achieve the unity that was needed to defeat Juárez in congress, Zamacona resigned as editor of *El Mensajero* though he continued to support Díaz and oppose Juárez.[34] The *juarista* press tried to help along disagreement by demonstrating that Lerdo had been the chief beneficiary of the alliance all along and that Díaz had gained nothing. They could also use Lerdo's earlier identification with the Juárez administration to remind *porfiristas* that assistance for Lerdo was support for the architect of some of the policies with which they disagreed. It was also clear that many of the leading supporters of Lerdo were opposed to threats of armed force if Juárez were elected and did not wish to be reminded that some of their allies in the *porfirista* camp were talking revolution.[35]

All in all, the three-way struggle had its points of humor.

Spokesmen for Juárez could not deny Lerdo's service to their own administration and could only try to identify him with the least popular decisions. By the same token, the *lerdistas* could hardly ignore their candidate's role in the ministry but had to blame Juárez for those policies they considered wrong and especially concentrate on actions taken after Lerdo's departure from the ministry. The *porfiristas* wanted to attack the administration but without alienating Lerdo or giving him too much credit. One result of the strange state of affairs was a reduction of much of the political propaganda to the level of personal attacks, rumor mongering and false charges.

Juárez's personal contribution to the campaign is difficult to assess. On the one hand he could use the power and prestige of his office to remind the people of his presence and his service without appearing to descend to the level of partisan politics. Still, he must have been privy to some of the decisions taken by *juarista* leaders in congress and in the states to assure his continuance in office. As he commented to one supporter after a legislative defeat: "It is one thing to legislate and another to enforce the laws. He who laughs last laughs best. . . ."[36] Juárez had also been involved in Mexican politics at all the various levels for too long to have been averse to the traditional manipulation of election machinery. His decision that it was best for the nation that he remain in office had been made, rightly or wrongly, and there is no likelihood that he ever seriously questioned the methods that might be required. He had even concluded that the possibility of armed revolt again was outweighed by the importance of his reelection. Neither he nor the other two candidates, however, appeared too obviously as the architects of their campaigns. Perhaps each was willing to "let the office seek the man," or have it appear so.

The outcome of the elections in June was no surprise to anyone, though all candidates claimed victory until the vote was counted. Whether because Juárez failed to use all of the force at his command and allowed a freer election than his opponents claimed or whether, in spite of fraud, force, and a small vote, there was stronger opposition than Juárez had anticipated, no candidate received a majority of the electoral vote. The final tally gave Juárez 5,837 votes, Díaz 3,555, and Lerdo 2,874. With no majority the election went to congress. Though the *lerdistas* had counted on just such an eventuality, by this time the congress had also changed its membership with a substantial increase in Juárez supporters; a simple head count showed what to expect when congress convened.[37]

The most serious question facing Juárez at this point while awaiting the convening of congress in September was whether or not a Díaz revolt was coming and when. Even more important was whether the *lerdistas* would join in such a military move. Félix Díaz had already made preparation for a revolt although his brother's position was as yet unknown. Romero, acting for Juárez, was busily engaged in urging a policy of conciliation. When the *lerdista* newspaper *El Siglo* finally rejected revolution as most *lerdistas* had always done, there was some relief but until the actual election was over and a new term underway, doubt would remain.[38] Even on the eve of the elections there had been a minor military mutiny in one of the Gulf ports; it had required bloody repression by the administration.[39] That this had been done without congressional authority could only raise the old specter of a dictatorial, repressive Juárez and might be a portent of things to come.[40]

The threat of a major revolt increased in September while congress was busy with organizational matters. Outbreaks occurred in Nuevo León, Sinaloa, and San Luis Potosí, and then on October 1 a truly dangerous uprising broke out in Mexico City when General Negrete and several other military men attempted to seize the Ciudadela. Though the rebels had spent a good deal of money, they were poorly organized and General Rocha crushed them rather speedily but not without a great deal of bloodshed and the unfortunate execution of a number of prisoners.[41] Here again not only was the threat of revolt against the government made clear but the degree of repression to which the Juárez military establishment had moved was all too apparent. Whether this would be a deterrent to other rebels or a cause only time would tell.

Finally on October 12 congress voted after almost a month of bitter debate over the credentials of deputies. Though the *juaristas* had the votes whenever needed, the opposition made full use of the opportunity to expose and denounce the illegal methods that had been used during the election as well as the whole procedure being used in congress. Although the *lerdistas*

were as strong as any in their criticisms of Juárez, they with-
held any support of possible revolution while some *porfiristas*
made it clear that any revolt that might come was clearly caused
by Juárez. The time came, however, for an end to debate and
the declaration of Juárez as the legally elected president. The
vote was Juárez 108, Lerdo 5, and Díaz 3, with the new term to
begin December 1.[42] Oddly enough, Lerdo remained as president of the Supreme Court with two more years to go of his six-
year term.[43]

The serious question as to what Díaz would do was answered
more quickly than some persons had expected. On November
8 the Plan of La Noria, calling for the overthrow of Juárez, was
published. This declaration, for which some of Díaz's supporters had been preparing since July, accused Juárez of dictatorial tactics, of rigging the elections with his own officials
backed by the military, of corruption in government, and of
general oppression of the people. Promising more liberty and
less government, Díaz adopted the standard of the Constitution
of 1857 as his motto and promised a new constitution.[44] The
revolt was necessary, Díaz claimed, because there was no other
way to remove the incumbent administration. In one of his
most ridiculous statements in light of later events, he proclaimed
that "if triumph crowns our efforts, I shall return to the peace
of my home, preferring in any event the frugal and tranquil life
of the obscure laborer to the ostentations of power."[45]

Though the proposed change in the constitution cost Díaz
whatever hopes he had of getting *lerdista* support, since their
own hero was next in line for the presidency if the constitution
went unchanged, the issuance of the Plan of La Noria created
substantial concern for Juárez. The declaration had not been
unexpected and Defense Minister Mejía had already taken steps
to defend the administration.[46] Nonetheless it would be a while
before the government could be certain of the extent of popular
support of Díaz and how effective military preparations had been.

By the middle of November Juárez asked congress to grant
him extraordinary powers to crush the rebellion. Díaz's backers
in congress tried a variety of parliamentary maneuvers without
success and on December 1, with some deputies still fearful over
earlier extensions of such power, congress approved Juárez's
request. In December and January the rebels suffered signifi-

cant losses, especially the seizure of Oaxaca and the capture and execution of Félix Díaz. By March Treviño met defeat in the north and Díaz's activities were reduced to nothing more than guerrilla warfare, with Díaz himself in refuge in Tepic. The final victory awaited the Lerdo administration that followed, but for all practical purposes the La Noria revolt was crushed by the middle of 1872.

Speaking with excessive optimism, Justo Sierra reports that "the moral authority of the government, having acquired new strength in the struggle, was now applied to a program for peace, . . ." This program involved education leading toward peaceful changes in government, the end of banditry, material progress, improved relations with Europe and increased foreign trade, domestic economic reform and education for the Indian and *mestizo* classes.[47] Granted these had been the earlier goals of Juárez and were no doubt still the ideals of which he dreamed, achievement was still as difficult and almost as far away as ever. An election victory tainted by government interference, a major revolt by a man as important as Díaz, the loss of support and prestige because of his ambition to remain in power, all were simply added to the existing fears and dislikes of Juárez and the congressional opposition to his program. Yet Juárez achieved some few victories in the months remaining to him and set the stage for much of the progress that would come under his successors.

The debate in congress over the extraordinary powers granted the president never really ceased and increased in intensity in April, 1872, when he asked congress for an extension. Juárez's personal defense of his past use of such authority did not remove the necessity for a fight, however, when the Minister of *Gobernación* proposed two laws in December asking for presidential power to suspend individual guarantees and an extension of the law on kidnapping and banditry. The latter was granted without much debate but the other provoked the usual storm of protest. Several alternative proposals were introduced by *porfirista* delegates that would have ended several suspensions of rights already in existence but they failed of passage. As he had done months before, Zamacona again argued that it was strange that the administration could not govern under the constitution and that so long as extraordinary powers were used anti-administration forces had no choice but to resort to revolt. In spite of the violence of the opposition, Juárez had the necessary votes and his desired legislation was passed on May 17.[48]

On other items Juárez was not so fortunate. In the last opening address that he was to deliver to congress the president again recommended two constitutional changes; first, the creation of a senate, and second, the revision of the constitution regarding presidential succession. The latter was clearly defensible in the face of occasions when both the president and vice-president died or were removed for unanticipated reasons. The senate, he had argued as early as 1870, was proposed "without any other purpose than that of assuring peace in the future on a solid foundation."[49] A senate, Juárez believed, would provide an improved legislative process and also be useful in resolving differences between the states, a power not provided for in the constitution. Congressional opposition still feared that the senate would simply be a presidential muzzle over the lower house and that its authority to intervene in state conflicts would increase executive control.[50] The result was that the congress refused to act on Juárez's recommendations. The failure of Juárez or congress to incorporate the laws of the Reform into the constitution might also be considered evidence of the lack of either presidential or congressional leadership, but the fact that the laws were being accepted in principle meant that little other than oratory was lost by this oversight.[51]

Insofar as economic legislation was concerned, it was Matías Romero once again who was primarily responsible for the proposals that were made and the efforts to obtain legislation. On April 2 he reported to congress on the existing financial picture and was able to report considerable advance in reducing expenditures, making payments on time, and collecting taxes more efficiently. He also reported a sizable new source of revenue for the government from contracts with minting houses, which were allowed to export gold and silver bullion. More importantly, Romero reported on a new tariff law promulgated by the president on January 1, 1872, and due to go into effect on July 1. By postponing its effective date, Juárez was allowing congress time to debate it and change it if the members saw fit. Several other changes effected by executive action were also reported.

Though Juárez's opposition had been eminently unsuccessful in passing their own laws, they were now able to demonstrate that they were strong enough to force changes in the administration's proposals. The tariff law became the chief subject under consideration; the budget introduced at the same time was inevitably affected. Congress even resorted to personal attacks upon the economic spokesman for the administration and accused Romero of having illegally or unethically profited from his government post. Romero asked for formal charges and a trial but congress preferred to simply continue the attack without exposing it to the necessity for proof. The tariff law was exposed to a large amount of discussion pro and con both in congress and the press, with part of the argument related to the economics of it and part to the politics of it.

The administration's tariff law, justified under the law of December 1, 1871, that had granted Juárez extraordinary powers in matters relating to the departments of War and Treasury, made few changes in tariff rates but did provide a number of other changes.[52] In general it simplified and codified the tariff schedule. It increased the number of items that could come into the country free of duty and abolished the list of prohibited items. The law also removed some of the restrictions that had existed upon the internal trade in foreign goods and allowed the export of gold and silver bullion. Article 19 of the law stated that states and municipalities could no longer charge import duties on foreign goods entering their jurisdiction, a provision that was certain to arouse anger, and the issue of allowing the export of bullion had earlier caused opposition. Most importantly, this time, as compared to earlier tariff proposals, the administration was proposing to take action by executive decree unless congress acted to prevent it.

The debate that followed Romero's presentation and the close margin by which the administration won parliamentary votes convinced *juaristas* that compromise was necessary if the overall tariff reform was to be preserved. In consequence, administration supporters introduced their own version of the tariff law. The significant changes included provisions for state taxes of not more than five percent on import duties and a repeal of the permission for untaxed exportation of gold and silver. Romero again appeared before congress to defend the administration's position. He first defended the president's authority under the law of December 1, 1871, and further pointed out that nullification of the tariff law would cause the government to lose faith in the eyes of those with whom contracts had already been signed. He then argued the virtues of the law insofar as it would provide the government with more revenue and stimulate foreign commerce by removing the uncertainties that had plagued merchants engaged in foreign trade.

As to the objections that had been raised, Romero explained that the law did not increase tariffs but simply combined them in a systematic manner. Objections to Article 19, he pointed out, were hardly valid since the constitution already stated that states could not tax imports without the consent of congress. The revised law would give this consent within the five percent limit and would in fact give the states as much if not more income than they presently received. Romero still felt it would be wise to allow tax-free exportation of bullion since the mining industry was the only base upon which the national economy could be built rapidly. In the long run he admitted that industrial growth was needed along with further efforts in agriculture but mining offered the greatest immediate advantages.

Always in the background of the tariff debate, as so much of domestic politics, had been the consistent issue of regional rivalries and needs. The tariff of 1872 was the first to take up the question of free trade versus protection as specifically as it did. The northern area, cities like Monterrey, felt the need for a free zone to aid their economic growth and were even willing to establish restrictions on the shipment of goods further south. The favored merchants of Veracruz opposed such equalization with Monterrey, however, and the central government feared the loss of customs revenue, whatever the virtues of concession to regionalism. A reasonable compromise to the Monterrey-Veracruz debate would not be found until after Juárez's death, but fortunately for him the more severe repercussions of the problem were postponed.[53]

The debate moved slowly in congress and by May the tariff had still not been approved. Because of the necessary relationship between anticipated revenues and spending, this meant also that the budget was not approved. Finally, on May 7, congress gave approval to the general budget but continued to debate specific items. On May 31, the final day of the session, virtually out of desperation, the budget of the previous year was simply extended for the next fiscal year. On the same day congress repealed Article 19 of the tariff and continued a small tax on the export of bullion.[54] The end result was not an administration victory but progress had been made in the sticky area of tariff reform.

A few days after the adjournment Juárez once again faced the task of selecting a new cabinet. The *pro forma* resignations that had been given shortly after Juárez's reelection had become official but the Díaz revolt and the coming congressional battles caused Juárez to ask the incumbent members to stay on. Once congress adjourned three ministers again submitted resignations: Mariscal, Castillo Velasco, and Romero. In selecting successors, Juárez offered Relations to José María Lafragua, *Gobernación* to Francisco Gómez del Palacio, Treasury to Francisco Mejía, and Justice to Joaquín Ruíz.[55] Lafragua, Francisco Mejía, and Gómez, along with most of the remaining cabinet members, were relatively unimportant men whose appointments caused criticism by the opposition and made defense by the administration difficult. Mejía, as Minister of War and the man responsible for some of the more repressive actions of the Juárez government, was hardly unimportant but he had become anathema to Mexican liberals. Only the proposal of Ruíz produced some pleasure for the opposition but it was short-lived since he refused the appointment after disagreeing with Juárez over the proper use of extraordinary powers. Ruíz believed that before the president used these powers, the approval of the entire ministry should be sought. Juárez, as he had done so often during his executive career, again defended presidential responsibility and authority though promising to consult with whatever ministry was directly involved. Ruíz thus refused the appointment.

With an uninspiring cabinet, Juárez had done nothing to alleviate the torrent of criticism that had been building ever since his reelection. His report to congress earlier in the year was combined with one of his increasingly rare public appearances and its content was little reminiscent of the man who had defied the French. "It was the voice of a magistrate tone deaf to the tension about him, the report of an official who had long since delivered whatever message he had for the world, and who had nothing within him to add to it. . . ."⁵⁶ Surely Juárez was tired; certainly he was ill. He suffered two minor heart attacks during the spring while the congressional battles were in progress. If he was aware of the state of the nation, which some of his opponents doubted, he knew that banditry and guerrilla activity had still not been ended. He could see easily that the financial problems of the republic had not been solved and that economic growth was much too slow to provide the jobs needed for a growing population. The old Indian from Oaxaca had not been able to provide the education he felt his people needed and had surely not freed them from the bonds of superstition. Relations with Europe had improved but little since the death of Maximilian and as a consequence increases in foreign trade had been meaningless. Most of all, Juárez had not led his country into an era of democracy and free elections for he himself personified the very evil of *personalismo* against which he had fought. There were many other minor failures he might have thought of and few real successes save the one great achievement —the creation of a Mexican nation that had endured.

Yet it was strange that a man who had won the hearts of his people, who had fought so diligently for the ideals of the reform and achieved some of them, would now be so vilified. That not one but many newspapers would call openly for his assassination would have been unthinkable even one year earlier. "Julius Caesar was greater than Brutus, and everyone blessed Brutus for killing him," wrote one and, "It being necessary to shoot Juárez out of the Presidency, we should resort to that method without delay," wrote another.⁵⁷ Even when sanity returned and the opposition rejected such horrors, the criticism was vile. "Don Benito Juárez is the Messiah of the owls and the crows," wrote one critic. "He is moving backward with giant strides . . . surrounded by pure Liberals in his period of triumph. Today he is calling the Moderates. Tomorrow he will be in the hands of the Conservatives." Then in unimagined prophetic words, on June 18, "there is something in the atmosphere that reeks of death."⁵⁸

One month later, on July 18, Benito Juárez died. Even his death encapsulated something of the stubborn, determined Indian origins of the man. Forced to leave for home by severe pains, Juárez was examined by his personal physician, Dr. Ignacio Alvarado, who found him suffering a severe heart attack. Though Juárez endured most of the examination on his feet he was finally forced to bed. At one point, after four or five hours of intermittent pain and conversation, his condition reached such a low point that boiling water was poured over his chest as a stimulant to the heart. It had the desired effect and Juárez revived sufficiently for his family to withdraw, and Juárez engaged in conversation with the doctor. Telling tales of his childhood, he at one point asked Dr. Alvarado directly, "Is my illness mortal?" When told that it probably was, Juárez casually continued his earlier discourse, only to be silenced by still another severe attack of pain. Once again the boiling water was applied, only this time Juárez bared his own chest and lay unmoving while the treatment was applied. "Not a muscle moved; not the slightest sign of pain or suffering; the body remained rigid, although a swelling several inches thick rose from the scalded flesh when the water dried."[59]

The end was not yet. The illness of the president was known but not its gravity, and the official family was not willing to make it known. Foreign Minister Lafragua, thinking the illness only rheumatism, insisted upon seeing the president. Juárez arose from bed, received the minister, and gave the advice requested. An hour later the process was repeated with a general who had come seeking advice for a campaign. Juárez not only gave advice but names of people to trust and other detailed information. Neither the minister nor the general were aware of the gravity of the situation and Juárez returned to bed. Sometime shortly before midnight with the doctor dozing, his heart stopped. Juárez had suffered the ultimate defeat that comes to all men.[60]

At daybreak the people of Mexico City were awakened by the roar of artillery followed by a gun fired each quarter of an hour, a sign of the death of the head of state. Following embalming and preparations, the body of the president lay in state for the procession of people to see. On the third day he was buried. Even now there were rumors of unnatural death, of poisoning at the hands of his enemies, and of charges that the ingratitude of the people caused a "broken heart." As one historian has commented, however, the "most widespread sentiment was probably relief at Juárez' passing."[61] If this is too strong a judgment there can be little doubt that Sierra, who admired Juárez, was right in assessing his death as "a national calamity, but at the moment it had one good effect, for it brought the civil war to an abrupt end."[62] But that is the story of what was to come; Juárez belonged to history and it was to be his total career and the way he lived his life that Mexico would remember. So long as his contemporaries lived, there would be the inevitable partisan attitudes. Once his generation had passed, the total effect of the man would be recalled, both for its good and its bad aspects. The symbol remained.

CHAPTER VIII

Epilogue

UPON THE DEATH OF JUÁREZ, THERE WAS NO DOUBT, FROM A LEGAL point of view, that Lerdo would automatically assume the presidency. He had been legally elected president of the Supreme Court in the election of December, 1867, and was therefore *ex officio* vice-president. Though he had to move cautiously to avoid possible *porfirista* opposition, that group's argument about "no reelection" was no longer valid and revolutionary sentiment dissipated. At the same time, Lerdo retained the *juarista* cabinet intact and avoided a possible continued break with the former president's supporters. The success of Lerdo's policies can be measured by the fact that he was almost unanimously elected president in the election held in October, 1872.

For the next three and one-half years Mexico enjoyed peace of a type practically unknown in the nation's previous history. The methods of government employed by Lerdo as well as the general legislative goals were essentially those of Juárez, not too surprising a fact in the light of Lerdo's major role in the previous administration. Partly because the stage had been set under Juárez and partly because of the simple passage of time, Lerdo could even claim somewhat more success in attaining legislation that had not been passed earlier. The overall thrust of the Reform had not changed, however, and it is clear that Lerdo's administration offered little more than a period of stabilization, of tying up loose ends, and of preparation for a new phase in the life of the nation—a kind of "era of good feeling."[1]

The brief period of relative tranquility that Mexico had enjoyed ended in the early part of 1876 when Díaz's continuing ambition for power found support from a number of militarists, a variety of discontented elements, and those who were attracted to the personality and glamor associated with Porfirio Díaz. The armed rebellion that broke out in support of Díaz was actually contained for a time by Lerdo and he was duly, and not surprisingly, reelected in elections held during the summer. The defection, however, of the new president of the Supreme Court, Iglesias, who had in some ways assumed the role under Lerdo that Lerdo had held under Juárez, was sufficient to bring Lerdo's regime to an end.

Thus began the Age of Díaz, a period of rapid economic growth with an increasingly dictatorial leader that would not end until 1910. Only with the coming of that great revolution would the Mexican government return to some of the goals associated with Juárez and add to them plans for even more extreme social change than he could have envisioned. For over thirty years it might have appeared that the only legacy Juárez had left his country was a precedent for prolonging the term of a chief executive and a political system under which only armed revolution could change the pattern and remove the curse of *personalismo*.

This is obviously too limited an assessment. Yet, how does one draw up a balance sheet on a man's life? Should a man be measured by his dreams or only by his concrete achievements? Do words mean anything or are actions all that count? Should Juárez be assessed by his contemporaries or by his successors —and which spokesmen in either category can be trusted? In reality, perhaps, the story of a man's life and public career should speak for itself, saying whatever it does to the observer. This is never the case, however, with any man who can be called a true "shaper of history," and various balance sheets have been drawn.

Clearly, those who worked with and against Juárez during his lifetime formed their judgments along partisan lines. They reacted to a human being whose policies or personality either attracted them or repelled them. It was easily possible for a Prieto or a Lerdo to switch from support to adamant opposition, and enemies could be won over. There can be no doubt that Juárez lacked the intellectual depth of some of his contemporaries and thus failed to appreciate fully the direction the Reform might have taken. He was a victim of ambition; he did succumb to the belief that his continuance in office, in direct contradiction to the constitution he so strongly supported, was a necessity. The prolonged imprisonment of Ortega and Juárez's treatment of lesser opponents was arbitrary and subject to honest criticism.

If, in spite of the charges that can be brought against the man, the Reform had achieved most of its desired results, his sins could be more easily forgiven. The Reform was a very incomplete success, however. True economic capitalism was far from realized; free elections were still a myth; equality before the law not only was not achieved, but conditions would worsen—in general, most of the ideals of the Reform had not been achieved. If these failures only are held up alongside the faults and mistakes of the man, Juárez's name would fade from history.

There was a time, during the Díaz dictatorship, when many authors did try with some skill to diminish the prestige and memory of the man whose name and reputation threatened the success and program of the Porfirian Era.[2] Fortunately, these attacks brought forth other studies of the Juárez period that produced a far more balanced appraisal.[3] The defense was so good that even the revolutionary attacks of the twentieth century upon Juárez for failing to have visions of far more radical change than he had, have done little to change the overall assessment of the man.

Even if all the criticisms of Juárez are accepted, and clearly some can be argued, there were successes for the Reform. The powers of the church, long obstacles to progress, were greatly reduced. An educational program had been started and, whatever its weaknesses, would continue to be an important part of any Mexican reform movement. The Indian, though not yet fully incorporated into the institutions of Mexico, had been given hope, and attention to his needs in the future was virtually inevitable. Under Juárez and Lerdo, at least, freedom of speech and the press were allowed and Juárez can hardly be blamed for the setbacks suffered under Díaz. Juárez's failure to accomplish more can be blamed in large measure on the nature and extent of the opposition that he faced rather than on his own inabilities. It is also true that his time was much shorter than his career in office would suggest. There was little opportunity for constructive programs during the War of the Reform and the French Intervention, not to mention the lesser military problems that challenged his administration. The tasks that Juárez set for himself were probably too great for any one person to accomplish in a lifetime. Indeed, one could argue that some of his ideals have not been achieved in a century under a series of competent leaders.

It is unfortunate that Juárez chose to run for his last term as president and added that act to the list of deeds his critics used against him. It is especially unfortunate since that campaign produced some of the most extreme vilification to which he had been subjected and his life ended at just such a time. It is more fitting that he be remembered for his total career and for the way he lived his life.

By his determination, even stubbornness, Juárez succeeded during the War of the Reform and the French Intervention in maintaining the symbol of the Mexican nation. It is probably not too much to say that his efforts created a Mexican nation. He not only won the respect of his own people but that of other nations as well. It is impossible to deny his dedication to the goals for which he fought. He seems always to have remembered his own origins and the hardships of his early years in Oaxaca. To provide justice and opportunity for others like himself was a guiding feature of his public career.

The continuing debate over whether the times or the man is more important can never be answered, but there can be no doubt that Juárez had as much influence on the history of Mexico as any single individual and that, on balance, his influence was beneficial. The designation by the Mexican government of the year 1972 as the "Year of Juárez" is a fitting testimonial to the security of his place in the history of Mexico, as well as the world.

Notes and References

CHAPTER I

1. This quotation as well as most of the information contained in this chapter on Juárez's early life will be found in *Apuntes para mis hijos,* an autobiographical sketch located in the Archivo Juárez (cited hereafter as AJ.), Biblioteca Nacional, Mexico City. It has been published in several places, including Jorge L. Tamayo, ed., *Benito Juárez, documentos, discursos y correspondencia* (14 vols.; Mexico: Secretaría del Patrimonio Nacional, 1964–1970), I, 24–273. Page numbers, where indicated, refer to the latter cited as Juárez, *Documentos.*

2. Harry Bernstein, *Modern and Contemporary Latin America* (New York: J. B. Lippincott Company, 1952), pp. 17, 22, 62. See also Herbert E. Priestley, *José de Gálvez, Visitor-General of New Spain, 1765–1771* (Berkeley: University of California Press, 1916).

3. Justo Sierra records that one had only to hear Juárez say "Señor Morelos" to realize the devotion that he and his generation had for the ideals of that great Mexican. *Juárez, su obra y su tiempo* (2nd ed., Mexico: J. Ballesca y Compañía, 1949), p. 32.

4. Act of Baptism, July 5, 1821, AJ.

5. This need for mastery of Spanish has been emphasized by almost all who have examined Juárez's career. See, for example, José C. Valadés, *El Pensamiento Político de Benito Juárez* (Mexico: Librería de Manuel Porrúa, n.d.), pp. 14–15.

6. Though unmentioned by Juárez, it is certainly possible that some less worthy motive determined the timing of his departure. Sierra claims that it was because he had just committed a "small theft of corn." *Juárez,* p. 32.

7. Louis Untermeyer, *Forjadores del Mundo Moderno* (Mexico: Biografías Gandesa, 1959), p. 142.

8. Sierra, *Juárez,* p. 39.

9. For a description of Juárez's seminary studies see Juárez, *Documentos,* I, 374–75.

10. The law providing for the Institute was actually passed on August 26, 1826, but obviously took a while for implementation.

Jorge Fernando Iturribarria, *Historia de Oaxaca 1821–1854* (3 vols.; Oaxaca: Ediciones E. R. B., 1935–1939) , I, 131.

CHAPTER II

1. Sierra, *Juárez,* p. 45.
2. Iturribarria, *Oaxaca,* I, 132.
3. Sierra, *Juárez,* p. 46.
4. Unless otherwise indicated, the information in this chapter is again based upon Juárez, *Apuntes.*
5. Oakah L. Jones, Jr., *Santa Anna* (New York: Twayne Publishers, Inc., 1968) , pp. 46–49.
6. Sierra, *Juárez,* p. 51.
7. Untermeyer, *Forjadores,* p. 144.
8. *Ibid.*
9. Jones, *Santa Anna,* p. 58.
10. Juárez, *Apuntes,* p. 135.
11. Charles A. Smart, *Viva Juárez* (New York: J. B. Lippincott Co., 1963) , p. 68–69.
12. Ralph Roeder, *Juárez and His Mexico* (2 vols.; New York: The Viking Press, 1947) , I, 67.
13. See for example the criticism of Sierra, *Juárez,* pp. 62–63.
14. Iturribarria, *Oaxaca,* I, 312.
15. *Ibid.,* pp. 304–305.
16. Smart, *Juárez,* p. 81, has Juárez resigning because León had drafted a protesting student into the army while Untermeyer, *Forjadores,* p. 145, attributes the rift to the governor's decision to enforce compulsory tithes. Both could well be true since a break over only one incident seems unlikely.
17. William H. Callcott, *Church and State in Mexico, 1822–1857* (Durham: Duke University Press, 1926) , pp. 70, 236, and J. Lloyd Mecham, *Church and State in Latin America* (Chapel Hill: University of North Carolina Press, 1934) , p. 403.
18. Jones, *Santa Anna,* pp. 64–79.
19. *Ibid.,* pp. 83–85.
20. *Ibid.,* pp. 91–96.
21. The third member of the triumvirate was Luis Fernández del Campo. Juárez, *Apuntes,* p. 145.
22. Jones, *Santa Anna,* pp. 101–10.
23. Other deputies to the federal congress from Oaxaca were Manuel Iturribarría, Tiburcio Cañas, Guillermo Valle, Manuel Encisco, and General Francisco Ortiz de Zárate. Iturribarria, *Oaxaca,* I, 139.

24. Manuel Dublán and José María Lozano, *Legislación Mexicana o colección completa de las disposiciones legislativas expedidas desde la independencia de la república* (34 vol.; Mexico: Imprenta del Comercio de Dublán y Chávez, et al., 1876–1904), V, 246–52. Cited hereafter as D y L, *Legislación*.

25. Wilfrid H. Callcott, *Santa Anna: The Story of an Enigma Who Once Was Mexico* (Norman: University of Oklahoma Press, 1936), pp. 225–57. See Michael P. Costeloe, "The Mexican Church and the Rebellion of the Polkos," *The Hispanic American Historical Review,* XLVI (May, 1966), 170–78, for a more complete account of the role of the clergy in planning and financing this revolt.

26. Angel Pola, ed., *Miscelánea de Benito Juárez* (Mexico: A. Pola, 1906), p. ix.

27. Roeder, *Juárez,* I, 82–83. Juárez, *Documentos,* I, 456–57, contains a defense of Juárez by Tamayo for assuming the governorship in 1847 at a time when cooperation with conservatives or failure was almost inevitable.

28. Roeder, *Juárez,* I, 79.

29. Juárez, *Documentos,* I, 468 69. For a more complete account of Juárez's governorship see *ibid.,* 443–804.

30. See for example Francisco de Paula de Arrangoiz, *Méjico desde 1808 hasta 1867* (4 vols.; Madrid: Pérez Dubrill, 1871–1872), II, 356, and Walter V. Scholes, *Mexican Politics During the Juárez Regime, 1855–1872* (Columbia: University of Missouri Press, 1969), p. 26.

31. Roeder, *Juárez,* I, 73; Bernstein, *Latin America,* p. 70.

32. Santa Anna, Mis memorias, García Collection, University of Texas. A published version of this manuscript appears in Santa Anna, *Mi historia militar y política, 1810–1874,* Vol. II of Genaro García, ed., *Documentos Inéditos ó muy raros para la historia de México* (36 vols.; Mexico: Librería de la Vda. de Ch. Bouret, 1905–1913). This will be cited hereafter as García, *Raros.* See *ibid.,* p. 46, and Smart, *Juárez,* p. 91.

33. Smart, *Juárez,* p. 94.

34. *Archivos privados,* p. 242.

35. Thomas Ewing Cotner, *The Military and Political Career of José Joaquín De Herrera, 1792–1854* (Austin: University of Texas Press, 1949), Chapters VI and VII.

36. *History of Mexico* (6 vols.; San Francisco: The History Company, 1881–1888), V, 557.

37. Bancroft, *Mexico,* V, 607–10.

38. Jones, *Santa Anna,* pp. 122–23.

39. Juárez, *Apuntes,* p. 165.

40. Juárez, *Documentos,* II, 8.

41. *Ibid.,* 9; Sierra, *Juárez,* p. 90.

42. Richard A. Johnson, *The Mexican Revolution of Ayutla, 1854–1855* (Rock Island, Illinois: Augustana College Library, 1929), p. 4.

43. Sierra, *The Political Evolution of the Mexican People* (Austin: University of Texas Press, 1969), p. 261.

44. Bancroft, *Mexico,* V, 628–49.

45. *Archivo Mexicano: Colección de leyes, decretos, circulares, y otros documentos* (6 vols., Mexico: n.p., 1856–1862), I, 5–9, and Juárez, *Documentos,* II, 13–15, both contain the text of the Plan of Ayutla. The amendments to the original plan provided for modification if and when the majority of the nation so expressed itself. The resolution was henceforth known as the Plan de Ayutla reformado en Acapulco. *Archivo Mexicano,* I, 10–18; Juárez, *Documentos,* II, 15–24.

46. Jones, *Santa Anna,* p. 131.

47. Ocampo to Juárez and reply June 13 and 19, 1855, in Juárez, *Documentos,* II, 48–49.

48. A good discussion of the moves made by the liberal leaders is in Johnson, *Ayutla,* pp. 100–110.

49. Text in AJ.

50. *Archivo Mexicano,* I, 57–59.

51. Juárez, *Apuntes,* p. 201.

52. Mecham, *Church and State,* p. 428; Callcott, *Church and State,* p. 70, f.n. 45.

CHAPTER III

1. Angel Pola, ed., *Obras completas de D. Melchor Ocampo* (3 vols.; Mexico: Imprenta de F. Vázquez, 1900–1901), II, 73–112, contains Ocampo's own account of his position during these days. This will be cited hereafter as Ocampo, *Obras.*

2. R. M. de la Torre to Manuel Doblado, October 24, 1855, in Genero García, ed., *La Revolución de Ayutla según el Archivo del General Doblado,* García, *Raros,* XXVI, 251.

3. For the law see *Archivo Mexicano,* I, 164–96. Walter V. Scholes, "Church and State at the Mexican Constitutional Convention, 1856–1857," *The Americas,* IV (October, 1947), 153, discusses the reorganization of the court system.

4. *Archivo Mexicano,* I, 129–31.

5. *El Heraldo,* December 13, 1855.

6. *Ibid.,* December 16, 1855.

7. *Ibid.,* December 23, 1855.

8. *Archivo Mexicano,* II, 110–44. See also Romero to Juárez, May 24, 1856, in Matías Romero Papers (Banco de México).

9. *Pensamiento Nacional,* December 25, 1855, cited in Scholes, *Juárez,* p. 6.

10. Justo Sierra, *Evolución Política del Pueblo Mexicano* (Mexico: La Casa de España en México, 1940), pp. 305–306.

11. José M. Vigil, *La Reforma,* in Vicente Riva Palacio, ed., *México a través de los siglos* (5 vols.; Barcelona: Ballescá y Compañía, 1889), V, 136–38.

12. Callcott, *Church and State,* p. 278.

13. Juárez, *Apuntes,* p. 249.

14. D y L, *Legislación,* VIII, 197–201.

15. Jan Bazant, *Alienation of Church Wealth in Mexico,* (Cambridge: Cambridge University Press, 1971), pp. 52–56.

16. The text of the constitution appears in *Archivo Mexicano,* III, 26–66, and Francisco Zarco, ed., *Historia del congreso extraordinario constituyente de 1856 y 1857* (2 vols.; Mexico: Imprenta de Ignacio Cumplido, 1857), II, 993–1016. The latter also contains accounts of many of the debates and the votes taken in arriving at the final document.

17. *El Heraldo,* May 11, 1857.

18. Juárez, *Apuntes,* p. 253.

19. Wilfrid H. Callcott, *Liberalism in Mexico* (Stanford: Stanford University Press, 1931), pp. 9–10.

20. D y L, *Legislación,* VIII, 431–32. This law became known as the Ley Iglesias after José María Iglesias, Minister of Justice under Comonfort.

21. Frank A. Knapp, *The Life of Sebastián Lerdo de Tejada* (Austin: University of Texas Press, 1951), p. 39.

22. *El Heraldo,* July 15, 1857, as well as other issues of that month.

23. D y L, *Legislación,* VIII, 650–51.

24. Oaxaca, October 24, 1857, in *El Heraldo,* November 1, 1857.

25. Text of Plan in Vigil, *Reforma,* p. 267. Manuel Payno, *Memoria sobre la revolución de diciembre de 1857 y enero de 1858* (Mexico: Imprenta de I. Cumplido, 1860), contains an account of the plotting that led to this action.

26. Vigil, *Reforma,* pp. 274–75.

27. *El Heraldo,* January 25, 1858.

28. Callcott, *Church,* pp. 84–96; Edward M. Caldwell, "The War of 'La Reforma' in Mexico, 1858–1861," Ph.D. thesis, University of Texas, 1935, pp. 1–7.

29. Caldwell, "La Reforma," pp. 121–26.

30. Roeder, *Juárez,* I, 161.

31. Vigil, *Reforma,* pp. 308–10.

32. Niceto de Zamacois in his *Historia de méjico* (18 vols.; Mexico:

J. F. Parres y Compañía, 1880, with a continuation by Francisco G. Cosmes published in 1901 in 4 vols.), XV, 296, states that of 61 major and minor encounters between the liberals and conservatives in the first half of the war, the liberals won only 16.

33. A description of these events is found in Prieto's poem, "Bello y sin par romance del 13 de marzo de 1858 de Guadalajara," in Pablo Prida Santacilia, *Siguiendo la vida de Juárez* (Mexico: Ediciones Palafox, 1945), pp. 94–97. See also Sierra, *Evolución Política*, p. 328.

34. *El Heraldo*, April 11, 1858.

35. Ocampo, *Obras*, II, 208.

36. Bancroft, *Mexico*, V, 742–44.

37. *Ibid.*, pp. 750–51.

38. Sierra, *Evolución Política*, p. 332, and Manuel Cambre, *La guerra de tres años en el estado de Jalisco. Apuntes para la historia de la reforma* (Guadalajara: Imprenta de J. Cabrera, 1892), pp. 214–16; 235–47.

39. Cambre, *La guerra*, pp. 416–417; 441–458.

40. See for example, S. Roel, ed., *Correspondencia particular de D. Santiago Vidaurri, Gobernador de Nuevo León, 1855–1864, Juárez-Vidaurri* (Monterrey: Universidad de Nuevo León, 1946), pp. 14–19.

41. Sierra, *Juárez*, pp. 155–63.

42. Degollado to Doblado, Tampico, July 4, 1959, in Carlos E. Castañeda, ed., *La guerra de reforma según el archivo del General D. Manuel Doblado, 1857–1860*, Vol. III in *Nuevos documentos inéditos ó muy raros para la historia de México* (San Antonio: Casa Editorial Lozano, 1930), p. 71.

43. Text in *Archivo Mexicano*, IV, 54–81, as well as in Ocampo, *Obras*, II, 113–42.

44. Knowlton, "Effects of Clerical Opposition," p. 256.

45. D y L, *Legislación*, VIII, 680–88.

46. Juárez to Vidaurri, Veracruz, July 14, 1859, in Roel, *Vidaurri*, pp. 20–21.

47. D y L, *Legislación*, VIII, as follows: civil marriage, July 23, 691–95; civil registration, July 28, 696–702; state control of cemeteries, July 31, 702–705; recall of legation, August 3, 705, and religious regulation, August 11, 762–66.

48. Cambre, *La guerra*, pp. 93–99.

49. D y L, *Legislación*, VIII, 658–61.

50. *Ibid.*, p. 663.

51. Ivie E. Cadenhead, Jr., *Jesús González Ortega and Mexican National Politics* (Fort Worth: Texas Christian University Press, 1972), pp. 24–25. Contrary to traditional practice with Spanish names this individual is usually referred to by his contemporaries as simply Ortega,

leaving off the patronymic. That usage has been followed in this study in the interest of consistency.

52. Juárez to Santacilia, Veracruz, July 12, 1859, in AJ. See also Juárez to Vidaurri, Veracruz, July 14, 1859, in Roel, *Vidaurri*, pp. 20–21.

53. McLane to Cass, Veracruz, April 7, 1859, in William R. Manning, ed., *Diplomatic Correspondence of the United States: Inter-American Affairs, 1831–1860* (12 vols.; Washington: Carnegie Endowment for International Peace; 1932–1939), IX, 1037–1044; 1050–1056; 1105–106.

54. *Evolution*, p. 291.

55. Manning, *Mexico*, IX, 968–69.

56. Cass to Forsyth, July 15, 1858, in *ibid.*, pp. 253–54. See also *ibid.*, pp. 969–99. For a brief general discussion of these events and those preceding and following, see Edward J. Berbusse, "The Origins of the McLane-Ocampo Treaty of 1859," *The Americas*, XIV (January, 1958), 223–45.

57. Manuel Payno, *México y sus cuestiones financieras con la Inglaterra, la España y la Francia* (Mexico: Imprenta de I. Cumplido, 1862), pp. 254–76.

58. Churchwell to Cass, Veracruz, February 9, 1859, in Manning, *Mexico*, LX, 1024–1030.

59. McLane to Cass, April 7, 1859, *ibid.*, p. 1043. See also Ocampo, *Obras*, II, 216–22.

60. Ocampo to McLane, July 9, 1859, Manning, *Mexico*, IX, 1101.

61. *Ibid.*, p. 1118.

62. *Ibid.*, pp. 1137–141.

63. Matías Romero, ed., *Correspondencia de la Legación Mexicana en Washington durante la Intervención Extranjera, Colección de Documentos para Formar la Historia de la Intervención* (10 vols.; Mexico: Imprenta del Gobierno en Palacio, 1870–1892), I, 216. Cited hereafter as *Correspondencia Legación*.

64. For one of the more severe criticisms of Juárez for his part in the McLane-Ocampo Treaty see José Fuentes Mares, *Juárez y los Estados Unidos* (Mexico: Editorial Jus, 1960). For a defense see Sierra, *Juárez*, pp. 192–99. A more recent apology for the treaty is Agustín Cue Cánovas, *El tratado McLane-Ocampo. Juárez, los Estados Unidos y Europa* (Mexico: América Nueva, 1956).

65. See Smart, *Juárez*, Chapter 13, for a more thorough discussion of the ship incident. See also Cass to McLane, April 28, 1860, in Manning, *Mexico*, IX, 284.

66. Bancroft, *Mexico*, V, 776–81.

67. *Archivos privados*, pp. 270–73.

68. M. Lerdo de Tejada to J. G. Ortega, Veracruz, July 23, 1860,

in González Ortega Papers (GOP), I, University of Texas. See Knapp, *Lerdo,* pp. 52–53, for a more complete discussion of Lerdo's role in these events.

69. *Diario de Avisos,* March 17, 1860.

70. Prieto to Doblado, June 26, 1860; Francisco Alatorre to Doblado and reply, July 9, 1860, in Castañeda, *Guerra,* pp. 188–92.

71. Sierra, *Juárez,* pp. 193–94.

72. José González Ortega, *El Golpe de estado de Juárez, rasgos biográficos del general Jesús González Ortega* (Mexico: A. del Bosque, 1941), p. 36; Cambre, *La guerra,* pp. 467–74.

73. Zamacois, *Historia de méjico,* XV, 467–69; Caldwell, "La Reforma," p. 203.

74. *Diario de Avisos,* August 21 and 22, 1860.

75. Hilarión Frías y Soto, *Apuntes biográficos del ciudadano-Jesús González Ortega* (Mexico: n.p., 1861), p. 43. (This work was published anonymously but is generally attributed to Frías y Soto. It will be cited hereafter as Ortega, *Apuntes.*) ; Bancroft, *Mexico,* V, 787.

76. Degollado to Ortega, August 29, 1860, in *"Don Santos Degollado, sus manifiestos, campañas, destitución militar, enjuiciamiento, rehabititación, muerte, funerales y honores póstumos,* in García, *Raros,* XI, 114–16.

77. Doblado to Degollado, September 10, 1860; Doblado to Echagaray, September 4, 1860; and manifesto of Degollado, September 12, 1860, in *ibid.,* pp. 124–27; 122, 117–21. See also Castañeda, *Guerra,* p. 243.

78. Scholes, *Juárez,* p. 41.

79. Bancroft, *Mexico,* V, 788; Ortega, *Golpe,* p. 43.

80. Degollado to Mathew, September 21, 1860, in García, *Raros,* XI, 130–33; *Diario de Avisos,* November 11, 1860. Roeder, *Juárez,* pp. 248–55, discounts the initial influence on Degollado by Mathew. He feels the entire affair was motivated by the psychological breakdown of Degollado when he realized the possible consequences of the seizure of the *conducta.* At the same time there is clearly the possibility that Doblado and Ortega had encouraged him, hoping that he would be discredited because he had been increasingly disliked in liberal ranks.

81. Degollado to Juárez, September 23 and 24, 1860, in AJ.

82. Unsigned letter of September 11, 1860, in GOP, II; Ortega to Degollado, September 30, 1860, in García, *Raros,* XV, 141–42.

83. Juárez to Degollado, October 4, 1860, in AJ.; Juárez to Ortega, October 4, 1860, in GOP, II.

84. Ignacio de la Llave, Minister of War, to Degollado, October

10, 1860, in Documentos Relativos de la Reforma, University of Texas; Llave to Ortega, October 10, 1860, in García, *Raros*, XI, 149–50.

85. Ortega to Nicasio Treviño, September 18, 1860, intercepted letter in *Diario de Avisos,* October 9, 1860.

86. Ortega to Degollado, San Pedro, September 26, 1860, in GOP, II. Juárez wrote on the back of this letter: "Degollado and González Ortega urge the president to give up his office." Fernando Ocaranza, *Juárez y sus amigos* (2 vols.; Mexico: Editorial Polis, 1939), II, 74.

87. *La Bandera Roja,* no date, cited in Cambre, *La guerra,* pp. 569–73; Luis Pérez Verdia, *Historia particular del estado de Jalisco* (3 vols.; Guadalajara: Tip. de la Escuela de Artes y Oficios del Estado, 1911), III, 112–13; Francisco Bulnes, *Juárez y las revoluciones de Ayutla y de la Reforma* (Mexico: n.p., 1905), p. 579; Ortega, *Golpe,* p. 46.

88. Ortega to Degollado, Belem, October 2, 1860, GOP, II.

89. Vigil, *Reforma,* p. 443; Ortega, *Apuntes,* pp. 47–50; Official report of Ortega to the Minister of War cited in Ortega, *Golpe,* p. 47.

90. Zamacois, *Historia de méjico,* XV, 521; Agustín Rivera y Sanromán, *Anales Mexicanos. La reforma y el segundo imperio* (Lagos: Tip. de V. Veloz, 1890–1891), p. 58.

CHAPTER IV

1. Porfirio Díaz, *Memorias 1830–1867,* (2 vols.; Mexico: Tipografía de la Oficina Impressora de Estempillas, 1922), I, 212; Rivera, *Anales,* p. 58; Juárez to Ortega, December 29, 1860, in Ortega, *Golpe,* p. 49.

2. D y L, *Legislación,* IX, 3–4; Vigil, *Reforma,* 446.

3. *El Monitor Republicano,* January 6, 1861.

4. *Archivo Mexicano,* V, 25.

5. *El Siglo Diez y Nueve,* January 16, 1861; *Archivos privados,* p. 277.

6. *El Siglo,* January 16, 1861.

7. *Ibid.,* January 17, 1861.

8. Ocampo to Sr. D. Luis Clementi, January 12, 1861, in *Obras,* II, 261, and Ocampo to Francisco Pacheco, Felipe Neri del Barrio and Francisco de P. Pastor, January 12, 1861, in *El Siglo,* January 15, 1861.

9. D y L, *Legislación,* IX, 12.

10. *El Siglo,* January 17, 1861; *El Heraldo,* January 20, 1861.

11. *El Siglo,* January 18 and 19, 1861; *El Heraldo,* January 21, 1861, and *El Pájaro Verde,* January 22, 1861.

12. Juárez to Doblado, January 20, 1861, Doblado Papers (DP). One is tempted to speculate as to what effect this may have had on Juárez's later decision regarding a pardon for Maximilian.

13. *El Siglo,* January 18 and 19, 1861.

14. *El Siglo,* January 21, 1861. Auza and Ogazón were both governors of states and had been suggested earlier by Ortega. Ortega to Doblado, January 17, 1861, in DP and Ogazón to Ortega, January 29, 1861, in GOP, IV.

15. Scholes, *Juárez,* pp. 60–61. See also the circular of F. Zarco, January 20, 1861, in Documentos para la Historia de México, Biblioteca Nacional, Mexico City.

16. Bazant, *Alienation,* p. 175.

17. *Ibid.,* p. 177. It may be that further research will prove that more economic reform was achieved than most writers believe, at least in specific areas. See Charles R. Berry, "The Fiction and Fact of the Reform: The Case of the Central District of Oaxaca, 1856–1867," *The Americas,* XXIV (January, 1970) , 277–90.

18. Bazant, *Alienation,* Chapters 5 and 6, contain as detailed an analysis of this complicated problem as seems possible.

19. D y L, *Legislación,* VIII, 760.

20. *El Heraldo,* January 11, 1861.

21. Ocampo, *Obras,* II, 144–46. See also *El Monitor Republicano,* January 23, 1861.

22. *El Monitor,* March 23 and 24, 1861.

23. Rafael de Zayas Enríquez, *Benito Juárez. Su vida, su obra* (Mexico: Tipografía de la Vda. de Francisco Díaz de León, 1906) , p. 116. See also Jesús M. Castañeda, Carlos Fernandez, and Rafael Díaz to Ortega, February 20, 1861, in GOP, IV. *El Siglo,* January 17, 1861, stated that a new paper, *El Porvenir,* was to be founded to support Ortega. On May 23, *El Heraldo* switched its support from Lerdo to Ortega.

24. Doblado to Ortega, January 4, 1861, in GOP, I; Ortega to Doblado, February 6, 1861, in DP.

25. *El Siglo,* March 14, 1861.

26. *El Siglo,* April 8, 1861. Miguel Galindo y Galindo, *La Gran Década Nacional, ó Relación Histórica de Reforma, Intervención Extranjera y Gobierno del Archiduque Maximiliano, 1857–1867* (3 vols.; Mexico: Imprenta y Fototipia de la Secretaría de Fomento, 1904–1906) , II, 35.

27. *El Heraldo,* April 2, 1861; *El Siglo,* April 6, 1861.

28. *El Heraldo,* April 6, 1861.

29. Ortega to Secretary of Relations, April 6, 1861, in GOP, IV.

30. Zarco to Ortega, April 6, 1861, in *ibid.*

31. Ortega to Zarco, April 7, 1861, in *ibid.*

32. Ortega, *Golpe,* pp. 58–60.

33. Ortega to Doblado, April 8, 1861, in DP.

34. *El Siglo,* April 9, 1861.

35. *Ibid.*

36. Ortega to Doblado, April 8, 1861, and Antonio Aguado to Doblado, April 8, 1861, in DP. See also Vigil, *Reforma,* p. 457, and Zayas Enriquez, *Juárez,* p. 117.

37. El Ciudadano Jesús González Ortega a la Nación, May 1, 1861, in GOP, IV.

38. José C. Valadés, *Don Melchor Ocampo, reformador de México* (Mexico: Editorial Patria, 1954), pp. 404–10; See also Vigil, *Reforma,* pp. 454–56, 460, and Ocampo to Juárez, May 4, 1861, in AJ.

39. Alfonso Teja Zabre, *Leandro Valle, un liberal romantico* (Mexico: Imp. Universitaria, 1956), pp. 117–26; Rivera, *Anales,* p. 67.

40. Sierra, *The Political Evolution,* p. 303.

41. Teja Zabre, *Leandro Valle,* pp. 127–43. See also Alfonso Teja Zabre, *Historia de México, una moderna interpretación* (4th ed., Mexico: Ediciones Botes, 1961), pp. 343–44.

42. *El Siglo,* June 8 and 10, 1861.

43. This address appears in *Documentos para la Historia de México,* Biblioteca Nacional.

44. Alejandro Villaseñor y Villaseñor, *Obras del lic. Alejandro Villaseñor y Villaseñor* (4 vols.; Mexico: Imp. de V. Agüeros, 1897–1910), II, 172–74; *Legislación,* IX, 233.

45. Felipe Buenrostro, *Historia del segundo Congreso Constitucional de la República Mexicana que funcionó en los años de 1861, 62 y 63* (Mexico: Tip. de F. Mata, 1874), pp. 73 ff.

46. Juan Ortiz Careaga to Doblado, June 12, 1861, José Linares to Doblado, June 14, 1861, in DP.

47. *El Siglo,* June 27, 1861; Zamacois, *Historia de méjico,* XV, 719.

48. *El Siglo,* June 18, 1861.

49. Ortega to his wife, July 1, 1861, in Ortega, *Golpe,* pp. 64–65.

50. Corwin to Seward, June 29, 1861, in U.S. *House Executive Document,* 37 Cong., 2 Sess., No. 100, 12.

51. Scholes, *Juárez,* pp. 73–75.

52. D y L, *Legislación,* IX, 248–50.

53. *Ibid.,* pp. 243–45.

54. See, for example, José Manuel Hidalgo y Esnaurrizar, *Un hombre de mundo escribe sus impresiones* (Mexico: Editorial Porrúa, 1960).

55. Sierra, *Evolution,* p. 305.

56. Cadenhead, *González Ortega,* p. 66; William Spence Robertson, "The Tripartite Treaty of London," *The Hispanic American Historical Review,* XX (May, 1940), 167–89.

57. Mexico, Secretaría de Relaciones Exteriores, ed., *Archivo Histórico Diplomático Mexicano* (Series I, 40 vols.; Mexico: Publicaciones de la Secretaría de relaciones exteriores, 1923–1936) , X, 24–28.

58. Dexter Perkins, *The Monroe Doctrine, 1826–1867* (Baltimore: The Johns Hopkins Press, 1933) , pp. 420–24.

59. *Archivos privados,* pp. 310–11.

60. Zamacona had been named to this post on July 13, 1861, in another cabinet revision. Others named at the time were Blas Balcárcel, Joaquín Ruíz, Zaragoza, and Higinio Nuñez. Bancroft, *Mexico,* VI, 18.

61. Text of treaty in *El Heraldo,* November 29, 1861, and Antonio de la Peña y Reyes, ed., *La Labor Diplomática de D. Manuel María de Zamacona como Secretario de Relaciones Exteriores,* Vol. XXVIII of *Archivo Histórico Diplomático Mexicano* (Series I, 40 vols.; Mexico: Publicaciones de la Secretaría de relaciones exteriores, 1923–1936) , 97–100.

62. Knapp, *Lerdo,* p. 72.

63. D y L, *Legislación,* IX, 327–28.

64. *El Heraldo,* October 3, 1861; Scholes, *Juárez,* p. 81.

65. Ortega to Minister of War, July 17, 1861, in GOP, V; Anto. Aguado to Doblado, September 8, 1861, in DP. See also Zamacois, *Historia de méjico,* XV, 723.

66. Ortega to C. Manuel Alas, Governor of Mexico, August 14, 1861, in GOP, V; Official report of the action at Jalatlaco by General González Ortega in Alberto M. Carreño, ed., *Archivo del General Porfirio Díaz, memorias y documentos* (2 vols.; Mexico: Editorial "Elede," 1947) , I, 265–69. Ortega and Díaz had some dispute over later accounts of the battle but Ortega did recommend Díaz's promotion to the rank of general.

67. *El Siglo,* August 20, 1861; *El Heraldo,* August 18, 1861.

68. See Ray F. Broussard, "Vidaurri, Juárez and Comonfort's Return from Exile," *The Hispanic American Historical Review,* XLIX (May, 1969) , 268–80, for a discussion of Comonfort's plans as well as other aspects of his relationship with Juárez.

69. Unsigned letter to Ortega, July 23, 1861, and M. Cabezuz to Ortega, July 25, 1861, in González Ortega Manuscripts (GOM) .

70. Speech by Ortega on taking possession of the presidency of the Supreme Court, August 20, 1861, in GOP, II; *El Siglo,* August 22, 1861.

71. *El Siglo,* August 23 and 29, 1861.

72. *El Siglo,* September 7, 1861; Ortega, *Golpe,* pp. 83–85.

73. *Archivos privados,* I, 303–305; Ortega, *Golpe,* pp. 75–76. See also Juárez to Doblado, August 29, 1861, in DP.

74. *El Siglo,* September 12, 1861; José Velazquez to Doblado, September 11, 1861, in DP.

75. Juárez to Doblado and Zaragoza to Doblado, September 13, 1861, in DP.

76. Ortega to Zaragoza, September 21, 1861, in *ibid.* Ortega had been named governor of Zacatecas in January and was still recognized as such in spite of his election to the court.

77. Two letters from Ortega to Doblado, September 23, 1861, in *ibid.*

78. Juárez to Doblado, September 28, 1861, in *ibid.*

79. Doblado to Ortega, September 29, 1861, in AJ; Ortega to Zaragoza, September 29, 1861, in GOP; *El Siglo,* October 2, 1861.

80. Felipe Buenrostro, *Historia del Primero y Segundo Congresos Constitucionales de la República Mexicana* (9 vols.; Mexico: Tipografía Literaria de Filomeno Mata, 1874–1882), III, 673–82.

81. Juárez to Lerdo, December 10, 1861, AJ.

82. *El Siglo,* December 10, 1861; *Archivos privados,* pp. 312–15.

83. Juárez to Doblado, December 5, 1861, in DP.

84. *Archivos privados,* pp. 313–14. The members were Doblado, Jesús Terán, González Echevería, and Pedro Hinojosa. Bancroft, *Mexico,* VI, 26.

85. D y L, *Legislación,* IX, 334.

86. This account of the background to the intervention and its first phases has been based primarily on the accounts in Egon Caesar Count Corti, *Maximilian and Charlotte of Mexico* (2 vols.; New York: Alfred A. Knopf, 1928), I, 98–176; Roeder, *Juárez,* pp. 318–423; and Bancroft, *Mexico,* VI, 21–44.

87. Juárez to Doblado, April 24, 1862, in AJ.

88. James Morton Callahan, *American Foreign Policy in Mexican Relations.* (New York: The Macmillan Company, 1932), p. 287.

89. D y L, *Legislación,* IX, 344–46; 350–52; 355–58; 364; 367–71; 423; 434–36.

90. Corti, *Maximilian and Charlotte,* p. 176; Bancroft, *Mexico,* VI, 42–48.

91. Díaz, *Memorias,* I, 241–67.

92. *El Siglo,* June 2, 1862. Ortega had been named constitutional president of the Supreme Court on May 31, 1862, as a result of elections which had been held during the last months of 1861, but had been serving as commander of the armies in Zacatecas, San Luis Potosí, and Aguascalientes up until this time. D y L, *Legislación* IX, 472; *El Heraldo,* February 23, 1862.

93. Ortega to Saligny, June 10, 1862, in AJ.

94. Ortega to Juárez, June 10, 1862; Juárez to Ortega, June 13,

1862; Saligny to Ortega, June 11, 1862, and Ortega to Juárez, June 17, 1862, in *ibid.*

95. Official Report of the Battle of Borrego by General Ortega, June 14, 1862, in Romero, *Correspondencia Legación*, II, 1181–1183; Official Report by Zaragoza, June 14, 1862, in *El Siglo*, June 17, 1862. See also U.S. *House Executive Documents,* 37 Cong., 3 Sess. (1862–1863) , No. 54, 147–49.

96. Scholes, *Juárez,* pp. 88–89.

97. Roel, *Vidaurri,* pp. 120–84; F. L. Owsley, *King Cotton Diplomacy. Foreign Relations of the Confederate States of America* (Chicago: University of Chicago Press, 1931) , pp. 118–39; Juárez to Santacilia, July 25, 1862, in Jorge Tamayo, ed., *Epistolario de Benito Juárez* (Mexico: Fondo de Cultura Economica, 1957) , pp. 172–73.

98. Justo Benítez, to Juárez, July 25, 1862, and Renato Zamacona to Juárez, July 19, 1862, in AJ.

99. *Archivos privados,* p. 324.

100. Bancroft, *Mexico,* VI, 53. A letter from José M. Patoni to Esteban Avila, January 31, 1862, in DP, mentions a rumor along this line. See also the exchange of letters between J. Terán and Doblado on August 13 and 14, 1862, in *El Siglo,* August 15, 1862.

101. Bancroft, *Mexico,* VI, 52–53.

102. Rivera, *Anales,* p. 97. There were at this time three Mexican armies. The other two were the army of the interior under Doblado and the army of the center under Comonfort, who had been allowed to reenter Mexico several months earlier. Broussard, "Vidaurri, Juárez and Comonfort," p. 279.

103. Galindo y Galindo, *Gran década,* II, 342–43; Ortega to Fuente, November 8, 1862, in Comonfort Papers, University of Texas.

104. Forey to Ortega, November 10, 1862, in AJ.

105. Telegram and letter from Ortega to Juárez, November 12, 1862; Juárez to Ortega, November 13, 1862; telegram from Ortega to Juárez, November 14, 1862, in *ibid.*

106. Ortega to Forey, November 16, 1862, in *Correspondencia Legación,* III, 96–97. The following day Juárez's approval was communicated by the Secretary of War. *Ibid.,* pp. 97–100.

107. The official report on the siege of Puebla was issued on September 16, 1863, in Zacatecas. *Parte general que da al supremo gobierno de la nación respecto de la defensa de la plaza de Zaragoza el C. general Jesús González Ortega* (Mexico: J. S. Ponce de León, impresor, 1871) . See also Cadenhead, *González Ortega,* pp. 71–72.

108. Much of the correspondence relative to the battle will be found in *El sitio de Puebla en 1863 según los archivos de D. Ignacio*

Comonfort y D. Juan Antonio de la Fuente, Vol. XXIII of García, *Raros,* and in the issues of *Diario Oficial* of the period.
109. Vigil, *Reforma,* p. 581.
110. *El Siglo,* May 29, 1863.
111. Bancroft, *Mexico,* VI, 71–72.
112. D y L, *Legislación,* IX, 623–25. The cabinet members then were De la Fuente, Terán, Nuñez, and Berriozabal. Comonfort replaced Berriozabal on August 18 and Doblado replaced De la Fuente from September 3 to 10, when he was succeeded by Lerdo. Terán resigned September 1 to be replaced by José M. Iglesias. Bancroft, *Mexico,* VI, 72.

CHAPTER V

1. Bancroft, *Mexico,* VI, 73–86.
2. *Ibid.,* p. 108.
3. Alcalde to Doblado, August 10, 1863, in DP.
4. The details of these exchanges are covered in various letters between Juárez and Doblado in AJ and in Scholes, *Juárez,* pp. 92–96.
5. *Archivos privados,* pp. 325–28. Lerdo seems to have been especially successful in working with Juárez and yet assuring Doblado that he did not like the situation. There can be no doubt that Lerdo played an important role in the next decade of Mexican history. See for example Scholes, *Juárez,* p. 98.
6. Rivera, *Anales,* p. 126.
7. Lerdo to Uraga, September 23; Lerdo to Juárez, October 1 and 2, in AJ and Juárez to Comonfort, September 28; Comonfort to Lerdo, November 1, and Lerdo to Comonfort, November 3, in Comonfort Papers. Also Uraga to Juárez, October, in AJ.
8. See for example D y L, *Legislación,* IX, 642–46.
9. Robert Ryal Miller, "Matías Romero: Mexican Minister to the United States During the Juárez-Maximilian Era," *The Hispanic American Historical Review,* XLV (May, 1965) , 228–45, is an excellent discussion of this important aspect of the Intervention.
10. D y L, *Legislación,* IX, 670–73.
11. Villaseñor y Villaseñor, *Obras,* II, 179, 187; Regis Planchet, *La cuestión religiosa en México ó sea vida de Benito Juárez* (Rome: Desclée, Lefeibvre y cia, 1906) , pp. 209–10.
12. Bancroft, *Mexico,* VI, 14–15.
13. Knapp, *Lerdo,* pp. 83–84.
14. Bancroft, *Mexico,* VI, 115–19; Ortega, *Golpe,* p. 156; *Archivos privados,* p. 25.

15. Vigil, *Reforma*, p. 620.

16. The members of the commission were Juan Ortíz Careaga and Nicolás Medina, representing Doblado; Martín W. Chávez, representing Aguascalientes and Trinidad García de la Cadena and Manuel Cabezut, representing Ortega.

17. Account of the conference in AJ. Letters had been written to Juárez advising him that the commissioners were on their way and urging him to resign. Chávez to Juárez, January 4, in *ibid*. On January 20, Juárez wrote both Ortega and Doblado advising them of his decision and restating his reasons. *Ibid*. See also Juárez to Romero, January 22, 1864, in M. Romero Papers.

18. Juárez to Doblado, January 20, in *ibid*. He referred to the escape of Ortega from the French at Orizaba. Even though Ortega had refused to sign the parole requested, some of the French felt that he had violated his word in escaping and taking up arms again.

19. Bancroft, *Mexico*, VI, 129: Knapp, *Lerdo*, p. 86.

20. Roel, *Vidaurri*, I, 259, 261–62; Scholes, *Juárez*, p. 104.

21. *Archivos privados*, p. 17.

22. Juárez to Ortega, March 14 and 15, 1864; Miguel Negrete, Minister of War to Ortega, March 16, Lerdo to Ortega, March 16, in Ortega, *Golpe*, pp. 205–206, 206, 206–208. See also Bancroft, *Mexico*, VI, 129.

23. D y L, *Legislación*, IX, 673–79.

24. Ortega, *Golpe*, p. 209; Bancroft, *Mexico*, VI, 130–31.

25. Bancroft, *Mexico*, VI, 125, 132–33.

26. *Ibid.*, VI, 149–50.

27. *Archivos privados*, pp. 337, 341.

28. AJ Manuscripts.

29. Rivera, *Anales*, pp. 151–52.

30. García, *Raros*, XX, 197, 120–26; Vigil, *Reforma*, pp. 644–45.

31. *Archivos privados*, pp. 342–48.

32. *Correspondencia Legación*, IV, 540–41.

33. Zayas Enriquez, *Juárez*, pp. 189–90; *Archivos privados*, pp. 346–49; Bancroft, *Mexico*, VI, 165.

34. Villaseñor y Villaseñor, *Obras*, II, 211.

35. *Archivos privados*, pp. 30–31; Jesús González Ortega, *The Presidency of Mexico* (New York: Russell's American steam printing house, 1866), p. 29. See also Galindo y Galindo, *Gran década*, III, 149, and Juan de Díos Arias, *Reseña histórica de la formación y operaciones del Cuerpo de Ejército del Norte durante la Intervención francesa, sitio de Querétaro y noticias oficiales sobre la captura de Maximiliano, su proceso íntegro y su muerte* (Mexico: Imprenta de Chávez, 1867), pp. 2, 190, for further comments on this battle.

36. *Political Evolution*, p. 320.

37. See Knapp, *Lerdo*, pp. 90–98, for more detailed description of the day-to-day business of the government.

38. *Ibid.*, p. 97.

39. Ortega to Lerdo, November 30, 1864, in *Correspondencia Legación*, IV, 559–561. See also *Diario Oficial*, December 3, 1864.

40. Article 80. This and other articles relative to the question will be found in Zarco, *Historia del congreso*, II, 1007.

41. Lerdo to Ortega, in *Correspondencia Legación*, IV, 561–65.

42. Ortega, *Golpe*, pp. 212–13; 223–24.

43. Negrete to Ortega, December 30, 1864, in *ibid.*, pp. 224–25.

44. *Archivos privados*, p. 35.

45. *Ibid.*, p. 36.

46. Díaz, *Memorias*, I, 369–412.

47. Tamayo, *Epistolario*, pp. 322–25.

48. September 15, 1865, in Juárez, *Documentos*, X, 184.

49. Margarita to mi estimado Juárez, November 10 and 15, 1865, in AJ.

50. Galindo y Galindo, *Gran década*, pp. 31–32.

51. Juárez, *Documentos*, IX, 754.

52. These instructions from Lerdo to Romero, December 30, 1864, appear in Romero, *Correspondencia Legación*, IV, 565–67.

53. Lerdo to Romero, January 26, in *ibid.*, V, 34.

54. Robert B. Brown, "Guns Over the Border: American Aid to the Juárez Government During the French Intervention," (unpublished doctoral dissertation, University of Michigan, 1951), discusses much of this.

55. Phillip H. Sheridan, *Personal Memoirs* (2 vols.; New York: Charles L. Webster and Company, 1888), II, 224–28.

56. Jones, *Santa Anna*, pp. 137–38.

57. *Ibid.*, pp. 140–48.

58. Juárez to Santacilia, March 30, April 27, May 18 and 25, June 8 and 15, and other letters during these months in *Archivos privados*, pp. 52–68.

59. This whole question of the presidency is summarized in I. E. Cadenhead, Jr., "González Ortega and the Presidency of Mexico," *The Hispanic American Historical Review*, XXXII (August, 1952), 331–46.

60. D y L, *Legislación*, IX, 717–18.

61. *Ibid.*, pp. 718–19.

62. *Ibid.*, pp. 709–21.

63. Article 82 of the Constitution of 1857.

64. The entire manifesto will be found in *Correspondencia Legación*, VIII, 464–89.

65. March 2, 1866, in *Archivos Privados*, p. 125.

66. *Ibid.*, pp. 121, 125.

67. Bancroft, *Mexico*, VI, 207–209.

68. *Ibid.*, pp. 225–29.

69. *Archivos privados*, p. 169.

70. Cadenhead, *Ortega*, pp. 113–17.

71. *Archivos privados*, pp. 207–208.

72. Knapp, *Lerdo*, p. 112.

73. Bancroft, *Mexico*, VI, 270–300; Sierra, *Political Evolution*, pp. 338–39; Díaz, *Memorias*, II, 103–52.

74. D y L, *Legislación*, IX, 367–71.

75. Knapp, *Lerdo*, pp. 114–16.

76. *Political Evolution*, p. 339.

77. *Archivos privados*, pp. 22–23.

78. Smart, *Juárez*, p. 387.

CHAPTER VI

1. *Political Evolution*, p. 341.

2. D y L, *Legislación*, p. 27.

3. Daniel Cosío Villegas, *Historia moderna de México* (8 vols.; Mexico: Editorial Hermes, 1955–70), I, 141–72, contains a discussion of this subject.

4. D y L, *Legislación*, X, 44–49.

5. *Diario Oficial*, August 22, 1867. Juárez was quick to see the error he had committed, but fought it out anyway. Juárez to Romero, August 28, 1867 in M. Romero Papers.

6. *El Siglo*, August 21, 1867.

7. *Ibid.*, September 9, 1867.

8. Guzman to Juárez, September 11, 1867, in AJ; *El Siglo*, September 23, 1867.

9. D y L, *Legislación*, X, 67–68.

10. *El Siglo*, September 13, 1867.

11. D y L, *Legislación*, X, 49–56. See also Knapp, *Lerdo*, pp. 126–28.

12. D y L, *Legislación*, IX, 689–90.

13. *El Siglo*, December 20, 1867; *El Globo*, December 19, 1867.

14. *El Siglo*, December 20, 1867.

15. See Cosío Villegas, *Historia*, pp. 183, 187, on election.

16. *El Globo*, December 2, 1867; Zamacois, *Historia*, XX, 126.

17. See various issues of *El Globo* through April, 1868.

18. *El Siglo*, February 27, 1868; *Diario Oficial*, April 23, 1868.

19. *El Globo*, June 6 and 9, 1868.

20. *Diario Oficial*, July 21, 1868. Patoni had been offered his freedom in September provided he would come to the capital and await

trial. He had refused his freedom unless it was unconditional, since he still considered Juárez to be holding office illegally. *Ibid.* See also *El Globo*, July 28, 1868.

21. *El Globo*, July 26 and 30, August 5, 1868.

22. Zamacois, *Historia*, XX, 213–26. See also Ortega, *Golpe*, p. 385.

23. Ortega to the Mexican Nation, August 19, 1868, in GOP, V, and *El Globo*, August 31, 1868.

24. *El Monitor Republicano*, November 7, 1868.

25. *El Siglo*, December 9, 1867.

26. *Ibid.*, December 11, 1867.

27. Scholes, *Juárez*, p. 124.

28. Elena Martínez Tamayo, "Un triángulo político," *Historia Mexicana*, I (July-September, 1951), 104–106.

29. Vallarta to Undersecretary of Foreign Relations, September 1, 1868, in *El Siglo*, September 4, 1868.

30. *El Siglo*, June 5 and 6, 1868.

31. *Ibid.*, September 10, 1868; *El Globo*, September 11, 1868.

32. September 11, 1868. It is noteworthy that by this time Zarco, a sometime friend of the administration, was fearful of a Juárez dictatorship and was opposed to some of its policies.

33. Zamacois, *Historia*, XX, 544–53. The law of January, 1869, appears in D y L, *Legislación*, X, 521–25. See Scholes, *Juárez*, pp. 127–29, for a further discussion of this subject.

34. D y L, *Legislación*, X, 24–25; 42–43; 65–66; 109–10; 278.

35. Zamacois, *Historia*, XIX, 418, 424–39; *Diario Oficial*, April 23, 1868.

36. Zamacois, *Historia*, XX, 22; Bancroft, *Mexico*, VI, 365–66.

37. Scholes, *Juárez*, pp. 125–26.

38. D y L, *Legislación*, X, 319–20.

39. *Ibid.*, p. 568.

40. D y L, *Legislación*, XI, 184. See Scholes, *Juárez*, pp. 129–31.

41. *Diario Oficial*, January 15, 1870.

42. Bancroft, *Mexico*, VI, 373–74.

43. Ortega to his fellow citizens, January 22, 1870, in Zamacois, *Historia*, XXI, 257–60.

44. D y L, *Legislación*, X, 29–30. See also Cosío Villegas, *Historia*, I, 74, 79–81; 84, 132–35.

45. *El Siglo*, August 7, 1867.

46. Sierra, *Political Evolution*, p. 345.

47. Cosío Villegas, *Historia*, I, 55.

48. Scholes, *Juárez*, pp. 131–33.

49. Zamacois, *Historia*, XXI, 37–39; Scholes, *Juárez*, pp. 133–34.

50. Sierra, *Political Evolution*, p. 347.

51. *Ibid.*, p. 346.

52. Various issues of *Diario Oficial* in April.

53. D y L, *Legislación*, X, 500–783; XI, 34–468.

54. *El Siglo*, September 23, 28–30, October 15, 18–21, 1868. The complete story of this railroad is told in David M. Pletcher, "The Building of the Mexican Railway," *The Hispanic American Historical Review*, XXX (February, 1950), 26–62.

55. D y L, *Legislación*, X, 88–94; 97–101; 137–43; 223–491, contains some of the legislation passed to implement the economic program.

56. Scholes, *Juárez*, pp. 141–48, contains a detailed analysis of Romero's whole program.

57. *Diario Oficial*, September 13, 1870.

58. *El Globo*, February 28, 1868. See Cosío Villegas, *Historia*, II, for a detailed study of the economy.

59. *El Siglo*, August 13, 1868.

60. *Ibid.*, November 11, 1867.

61. *Ibid.*, December 23–26, 1868.

62. Cosmes, *Historia*, XXI, 39–50.

63. *Ibid.*, XX, 874–86.

64. Roeder, *Juárez*, II, 716.

65. Sierra, *Political Evolution*, p. 348.

66. Scholes, *Juárez*, pp. 138–39. See Albert J. Delmez, "The Positivist Philosophy in Mexican Education, 1867–1873," *The Americas*, VI (July, 1949), 1, for a more thorough discussion. The prolific writings of Leopoldo Zea, especially *El positivismo en México* (Mexico, El Colegio de México, 1943), still represent the best sources of information on positivism in Mexico although William D. Raat, "Leopoldo Zea and Mexican Positivism: A Reappraisal," *The Hispanic American Historical Review*, XLVIII, (February, 1968), 1–18, provides a cogent criticism of Zea without denying his importance.

67. D y L, *Legislación*, X, 193–205.

68. Knapp, *Lerdo*, p. 120.

CHAPTER VII

1. Lerdo to Minister of *Gobernación*, January 14, 1871, in *El Siglo*, January 18, 1871.

2. Lerdo to Mariano Riva Palacio, September 22, 1870, in M. Riva Palacio Papers, University of Texas.

3. Cosmes, *Historia*, XXI, 745–57.

4. See Cosío Villegas, *Historia*, I, 212–16, for a further discussion of this resignation.

5. Knapp, *Lerdo*, p. 150.

6. Zayas Enriquez, *Juárez*, p. 236.
7. Manuel Saavedra to Lerdo, January 17, 1871, in *El Siglo*, January 18, 1871.
8. Knapp, *Lerdo*, p. 152.
9. Mejía to M. Riva Palacio, January 26, 1871, in M. Riva Palacio Papers.
10. Knapp, *Lerdo*, p. 153.
11. Scholes, *Juárez*, p. 151.
12. *El Siglo*, January 18, 1871.
13. Knapp, *Lerdo*, p. 153.
14. *Ibid.*
15. Scholes, *Juárez*, p. 151 and Knapp, *Lerdo*, p. 154.
16. Cosmes, *Historia*, XXI, 761–64; *El Siglo*, February 2 and 4, 1871.
17. *El Siglo*, January 13 and 14, 1871.
18. Knapp, *Lerdo*, p. 152.
19. Walter V. Scholes, "*El Mensajero* and the Election of 1871," *The Americas*, V (July, 1948), 61–67, is a summary of the program as well as the policies of the paper.
20. Knapp, *Lerdo*, pp. 152–53.
21. *Ibid.*, p. 158, n. 138.
22. *Archivo Díaz*, IX, 143–56.
23. Scholes, *Juárez*, p. 156; Cosmes, *Historia*, XXI, 969–70.
24. Cosmes, *Historia*, XXI, 735–57.
25. Scholes, *Juárez*, pp. 154–55.
26. D y L, *Legislación*, XI, 495–98.
27. *Diario Oficial*, May 12 and 13, 1871.
28. Cosmes, *Historia*, XXI, 916–929.
29. Scholes, *Juárez*, pp. 157–58.
30. Cosmes, *Historia*, XXI, 524–76; 795–808; 849; 994–95; 1038.
31. *Diario Oficial*, June 11 and 14, 1871.
32. Scholes, *Juárez*, pp. 158–59.
33. *El Siglo*, April 19, 1871; Zamacona to Díaz, June, 1871, in *Archivo Díaz*, IX, 143–56.
34. Scholes, *Juárez*, p. 158.
35. *El Siglo*, May 11 and various other issues during the campaign.
36. Cosmes, *Historia*, XXI, 970.
37. *Ibid.*, XXII, 19–20.
38. Scholes, *Juárez*, pp. 160–61.
39. Angel Miranda Basurto, *La Evolución de México* (Mexico: Editorial Herrero, 1959), p. 273.
40. *Political Evolution*, p. 350.
41. Smart, *Juárez*, p. 411.
42. *Ibid.*

43. Knapp, *Lerdo,* p. 158.

44. Cosmes, *Historia,* XXII, 54–62.

45. *Ibid.,* pp. 59–60.

46. Mejía to M. Riva Palacio, August 11 and 12, 1871, in M. Riva Palacio Papers as well as several other letters written in October.

47. Sierra, *Political Evolution,* p. 352.

48. Scholes, *Juárez,* Chapter VIII, is one of the few adequate sources on Juárez's last term in office and unless otherwise indicated is the source used here. Scholes in turn relied heavily on the debates in the congress.

49. Juárez to M. Riva Palacio, April 15, 1870, in M. Riva Palacio Papers. See also April 22, 1870.

50. See, for example, the provisions of the law that finally did create the senate in 1874. D y L, *Legislación,* XII, 639.

51. Knapp, *Lerdo,* p. 189.

52. D y L, *Legislación,* XII, 6–87.

53. Bernstein, *Latin America,* pp. 84–87. Another example of this extreme regionalism developed when the businessmen of Colima sought the support of Guadalajara to push construction of a railroad there and the development of the Pacific port at Manzanillo as a counter to the economic dominance of the central and Gulf cities. *Ibid.,* p. 90, f.n. 17.

54. *Ibid.,* p. 202.

55. *Diario Oficial,* June 10, 1872.

56. Roeder, *Juárez,* II, 723.

57. Cited in *ibid.,* p. 724.

58. *Ibid.*

59. *Ibid.,* p. 725. A detailed account of Juárez's death will be found in Cosmes, *Historia,* XXII, 304–50.

60. Smart, *Juárez,* 416–17.

61. Knapp, *Lerdo,* p. 159.

62. *Political Evolution,* p. 352.

EPILOGUE

1. See Knapp, *Lerdo,* Chapter IX, for a convincing and laudatory account of the Lerdo administration.

2. See, for example, Francisco Bulnes, *El verdadero Juárez y la verdad sobre la intervención y el imperio* (Mexico: La vda. de C. Bouret, 1904).

3. See, for example, Sierra, *Juárez.*

Selected Bibliography

PRIMARY SOURCES

Manuscript Materials

Archivo Juárez, Biblioteca Nacional, Mexico City.
Bancroft Papers, University of California (Berkeley).
Ignacio Comonfort Papers, University of Texas (Austin).
Santos Degollado Papers, Texas.
Manuel Doblado Papers, Texas.
Documentos relativos a la reforma, Texas.
Jesús González Ortega Manuscripts, Texas.
Jesús González Ortega Papers, Texas.
Mariano Riva Palacio Papers, Texas.
Vicente Riva Palacio Papers, Texas.
Matías Romero Papers, Banco de México.
Jesús Terán Typescripts, Texas.
Plácido Vega Papers, California.

Printed Documents and Correspondence

Archivo Mexicano: Colección de leyes, decretos, circulares, y otros documentos. 6 vols. Mexico: no publisher, 1856–1862.
British and Foreign State Papers. Vols. XLIV–XLVI. London: William Ridgway, 1860–1862.
Buenrostro, Felipe. *Historia del primero y segundo congreso constitucionales de la república mexicana.* 9 vols. Mexico: Tipografía Literaria de Filomeno Mata, 1874–1882.
———. *Historia del segundo congreso constitucional de la República Mexicana, que funcionó en los años de 1861, 62 y 63.* Mexico: Tip de F. Mata, 1874.
Carreño, Alberto M. (ed.). *Archivo del General Porfirio Díaz, memorias y documentos.* 10 vols. Mexico: Editorial "Elede," 1947–1951.
Castañeda, Carlos E. (ed.). *La guerra de reforma según el archivo del General D. Manuel Doblado, 1857–1860.* Vol. III of *Nuevos docu-*

mentos inéditos ó muy raros para la historia de Mexico. San Antonio: Casa Editorial Lozano, 1930.

Colección de leyes, decretos y circulares expedidas por el supremo gobierno de la república, 1863–1867. 3 vols. Mexico: Imprenta del Gobierno en Palacio, 1867.

Dublán, Manuel and Lozano, José María (eds.). *Legislación mexicana ó colección completa de las disposiciones legislativas expedidas desde la independencia de la república.* 34 vols. Mexico: Imprenta del Comercio de Dublán y Chávez, et al., 1876–1904.

García, Genero (ed.). *Documentos inéditos ó muy raros para la historia de México.* 36 vols. Mexico: Librería de la Vda. de Ch. Bouret, 1905–193.

Especially:

Vol. II. Santa Anna. *Mi historia militar y política, 1810–1874: Memorias inéditos.* Vol. XI. *Don Santos Degollado, sus manifiestos, campañas, destitución militar, enjuiciamiento, rehabilitación, muerte, funerales y honores postumos.* Vol. XXIII. *El sitio de Puebla en 1863 según los archivos de D. Ignacio Comonfort y D. Juan Antonio de la Fuente.* Vol. XXVI. *La revolución de Ayutla según el archivo del General Doblado.*

González Ortega, Jesús. *Parte general que da al supremo gobierno de la nación respecto de la defensa de la plaza de Zaragoza el C. general Jesús González Ortega.* Mexico: J. S. Ponce de León, impresor, 1871.

Gutiérrez, Blas José, and Alatorre, Flores (eds.). *Leyes de reforma colección de las disposiciones que se conocen con este nombre publicadas desde el año de 1855 al de 1870.* 2 vols. Mexico: Miguel Zornoza, Impresor, 1868–1870.

Hernández Rodríguez, Rosaura. *Ignacio Comonfort Trayectoria Politica. Documentos.* Mexico: Universidad Nacional Autónoma de México, 1967.

Manning, William R. (ed.). *Diplomatic Correspondence of the United States: Inter-American Affairs, 1831–1860,* 12 vols. Washington: Carnegie Endowment for International Peace, 1932–1939.

Mexico, Secretaría de Relaciones Exteriores (ed.). *Archivo Histórico Diplomatico Mexicano.* Series I, 40 vols. Mexico: Publicaciones de la Secretaría de relaciones exteriores, 1923–1936.

Pérez Lugo, J. *La cuestión religiosa en Mexico, recopilación de leyes, disposiciones legales y documentos para el estudio de este problema político.* Mexico: Publicaciones del Centro Cultural "Cuauhtemoc," 1926.

Pola, Angel (ed.). *Obras completas de D. Melchor Ocampo.* 3 vols. Mexico: Imprenta de F. Vázquez, 1900–1901.

Puig Casauranc, J. M. (ed.). *Archivos privados de Benito Juárez y D. Pedro Santacilia.* Mexico: Secretaría de Educación Pública, 1928.
Roel, S. (ed.). *Correspondencia particular de D. Santiago Vidaurri, Gobernador de Nuevo León, 1855–1864.* Monterrey: Universidad de Nuevo León, 1946.
Romero, Matías (ed.). *Correspondencia de la legación mexicana en Washington durante la intervención, extranjera, colección de documentos para formar la historia de la intervención.* 10 vols. Mexico: Imprenta del Gobierno en Palacio, 1870–1892.
———. *Archivo Histórico de Matías Romero.* Edited by Guadalupe Monroy. Vol. I. Mexico: Banco de México, S.A., 1965.
Ruíz, Manuel. *Exposición que el C. Lic. Manuel Ruiz, ministro constitucional de la suprema corte de justicia de la nación, presenta al soberano congreso de la union.* Mexico: Imprenta de Nabor Chávez, 1868.
Tamayo, Jorge L. (ed.). *Benito Juárez, documentos, discursos y correspondencia.* 14 vols. Mexico: Secretaría del Patrimonio Nacional, 1964–1970.
———. *Epistolario de Benito Juárez.* Mexico: Fondo de Cultura Económica, 1957.
United States *House Executive Documents.*
No. 100, 37 Cong., 2 Sess. Washington, 1862.
No. 120, 37 Cong., 2 Sess. Washington, 1862.
No. 54, 37 Cong., 3 Sess. Washington, 1863.
No. 73, 39 Cong., 1 Sess. Washington, 1866.
No. 1, 39 Cong., 2 Sess. Washington, 1867.
No. 17, 39 Cong., 2 Sess. Washington, 1867.
No. 76, 39 Cong., 2 Sess. Washington, 1867.
No. 30, 40 Cong., 1 Sess. Washington, 1867.
No. 1, 40 Cong., 2 Sess. Washington, 1867.
United States *Papers Relating to Foreign Relations.*
39 Cong., 2 Sess., III. Washington, 1867.
40 Cong., 2 Sess., II. Washington, 1868.
War of the Rebellion. Vols. XXXIV, XLI. Washington: Government Printing Office, 1891, 1893.
Zarco, Francisco (ed.). *Historia del congreso extraordinario constituyente de 1856 y 1857.* 2 vols. Mexico: Imprenta de Ignacio Cumplido, 1857.

Contemporary Accounts

Arias, Juan de Díos. *Reseña histórica de la formación y operaciones del cuerpo de ejército del norte durante la intervención francesa, sitio de Querétaro y noticias oficiales sobre la captura de*

Maximiliano, su proceso íntegro y su muerte. Mexico: Imprenta de Chávez, 1867.

Blasio, José L. *Maximilian Emperor of Mexico: Memoirs of His Private Secretary.* New Haven: Yale University Press, 1934.

Bulnes, Francisco. *Juárez y las revoluciones de Ayutla y de la Reforma.* Mexico: no publisher, 1905.

——. *El verdadero Juárez y la verdad sobre la intervención y el imperio.* Mexico: La vda. de C. Bouret, 1904.

Díaz, Porfirio. *Memorias, 1830–1867.* 3 vols. Mexico: Tipografía de la Oficina Impresora de Estampillas, 1922.

Foster, John W. *Diplomatic Memoirs.* 2 vols. Boston: Houghton, 1909.

González Ortega, Jesús. *The Presidency of Mexico.* New York: Russell's American steam printing house, 1866.

Payno, Manuel. *Memoria sobre la revolución de diciembre de 1857 y enero de 1858.* Mexico: Imprenta de I. Cumplido, 1860.

——. *México y sus cuestiones financieras con la Inglaterra y la Francia.* Mexico: Imprenta de I. Cumplido, 1862.

Portilla, Anselmo de la. *Méjico en 1856 y 1857, gobierno de General Comonfort.* New York: Imprenta de S. Hallet, 1858.

Prieto, Guillermo. *Lecciones de historia patria escritas para los alumnos del colegio militar.* Mexico: Oficina Tip. de la Secretaría Fomento, 1891.

——. *Memorias de mis tiempos 1840 a 1853.* Mexico: Librería de la Vda. de C. Bouret, 1906.

Sheridan, Philip H. *Personal Memoirs.* 2 vols. New York: Charles L. Webster and Company, 1888.

Sierra, Justo. *Evolución Política del Pueblo Mexicano.* Mexico: La Casa de España en México, 1940.

——. *Juárez, su obra y su tiempo.* Mexico: J. Ballesca y Compañía, 1905–1906.

——. *The Political Evolution of the Mexican People.* Edited by Edmundo O'Gorman. Translated by Charles Ramsdell. Austin: University of Texas Press, 1969.

Vigil, José M. *La Reforma.* Vol. V of Riva Palacio, Vicente (ed.). *México a través de los siglos.* 5 vols. Barcelona: Ballesca y Compañía, 1889.

Zamacois, Niceto de. *Historia de méjico desde sus tiempos más remotos hasta nuestros días.* 18 vols. Mexico: J. F. Parres y Compañía, 1880, with a continuation by Cosmes, Francisco G. 4 vols. 1901.

Zayas Enríquez, Rafael de. *Benito Juárez—su vida su obra.* Mexico: Tipografía de la Vda. de Francisco Díaz de León, 1906.

——. *Porfirio Díaz.* Trans. by T. Quincy Browne, Jr. New York: D. Appleton and Company, 1908.

Newspapers and Periodicals
(Mexico City unless otherwise stated)

El Boletín de Noticias, 1860–1861.
El Defensor de la Reforma (Zacatecas), 1864.
Diario de Avisos, 1856–1860.
El Diario del Imperio, 1865–1866.
Diario oficial (including *Periódico Oficial* of the Intervention Period), 1863–1872.
El Estandarte Nacional, 1856–1857.
El Globo de México, 1867–1869.
El Heraldo, 1854–1863.
El Monitor Republicano, 1868–1872.
El Pájaro Verde, 1861–1866.
El Siglo Diez y Nueve, 1858–1863.
La Soberanía de Tamaulipas (Tampico), 1866.

SECONDARY SOURCES

Books

Arrangoiz, Francisco de Paula de. *México desde 1808 hasta 1867* 4 vols. Madrid: Pérez Dubrill, 1871–1872.
Arrowood, Flora R. "United States-Mexican Foreign Relations from 1867–1872." M.A. thesis, University of Texas, 1934.
Bancroft, Hubert H. *History of Mexico*. 6 vols. San Francisco: The History Company, 1881–1888.
Bazant, Jan. *Alienation of Church Wealth in Mexico*. Cambridge: Cambridge University Press, 1971.
Beals, Carleton. *Porfirio Díaz, Dictator of Mexico*. Philadelphia: Lippincott, 1932.
Bernstein, Harry. *Modern and Contemporary Latin America*. New York: J. B. Lippincott Company, 1952.
Bravo Ugarte, José. *Historia de México*. Vol. III. Mexico: Editorial Jus, 1944.
Brown, Robert B. "Guns Over the Border: American Aid to the Juárez Government During the French Intervention." Ph.D. thesis, University of Michigan, 1951.
Burke, Ulick Ralph. *A Life of Benito Juárez, Constitutional President of Mexico*. London: Remington and Company, Ltd., 1894.
Cadenhead, Jr., Ivie E. *Jesús González Ortega and Mexican National Politics*. Fort Worth: Texas Christian University Press, 1972.

Caldwell, Edward M. "The War of 'La Reforma' in Mexico, 1858–1861." Ph.D. thesis, University of Texas, 1935.

Callahan, James Morton. *American Foreign Policy in Mexican Relations.* New York: The Macmillan Company, 1932.

Callcott, Wilfrid H. *Church and State in Mexico, 1822–1857,* Durham: Duke University Press, 1926.

——. *Liberalism in Mexico.* Stanford: Stanford University Press, 1931.

——. *Santa Anna, The Story of an Enigma Who Once Was Mexico.* Norman: University of Oklahoma Press, 1936.

Cambre, Manuel. *La guerra de tres años en el estado de Jalisco. Apuntes para la historia de la reforma.* Guadalajara: Imprenta de J. Cabrera, 1892.

Corti, Count Egon Caesar. *Maximilian and Charlotte of Mexico.* 2 vols. New York: Alfred A. Knopf, 1928.

Cosío Villegas, Daniel. *Historia moderna de México.* 8 vols. Mexico: Editorial Hermes, 1955–1970.

——. *La historiografía política del México moderno.* Mexico: El Colegio Nacional, 1953.

Cotner, Thomas Ewing. *The Military and Political Career of José Joaquín De Herrera, 1792–1854.* Austin: University of Texas Press, 1949.

Cue Cánovas, Agustín. *La reforma liberal en México.* Mexico: Ediciones Centenario, 1960.

——. *El tratado McLane-Ocampo. Juárez, los Estados Unidos y Europa.* Mexico: América Neuva, 1956.

Cuevas, Mariano. *Historia de la nación mexicana.* Mexico: Talleres Tipográficos Modelo, 1940.

Diffie, Bailey W. *Latin American Civilization.* Harrisburg: Stackpole Sons, 1945.

Fuentes Mares, José. *Juárez y los Estados Unidos.* Mexico: Editorial Jus, 1964.

——. *Juárez y el imperio.* Mexico: Editorial Jus, 1963.

——. *Juárez y la intervención.* Mexico: Editorial Jus, 1962.

——. *Juárez y la republica.* Mexico: Editorial Jus, 1965.

Galindo y Galindo, Miguel. *La gran década nacional, ó relación histórica de la guerra de reforma, intervención extranjera y gobierno del Archiduque Maximiliano, 1857–1867.* 3 vols. Mexico: Imprenta y Fototipia de la Secretaría de Fomento, 1904–1906.

García, Genero. *Juárez, refutación a Don Francisco Bulnes.* Mexico: Bouret, 1904.

García Granados, R. *Historia de México desde la restauración de la republica en 1867, hasta la caída de Porfirio Díaz.* 4 vols. Mexico: Librería Editorial de Andrés Botas e Hijo, ?–1928.

González Ortega, José. *El golpe de estado de Juárez, rasgos biográficos del general Jesús González Ortega.* Mexico: A del Bosque, impresor, 1941.

Hidalgo y Esnaurrizar, José Manuel. *Un hombre de mundo escribe sus impresiones.* Mexico: Editorial Porrúa, 1960.

Iturribarria, Jorge Fernando. *Historia de Oaxaca.* 3 vols. Oaxaca: Ediciones E.R.B., 1935–39.

Johnson, Richard A. *The Mexican Revolution of Ayutla, 1854–1855.* Rock Island, Illinois: Augustana College Library, 1939.

Jones, Jr., Oakah L. *Santa Anna.* New York: Twayne Publishers, Inc., 1968.

Knapp, Frank A. *The Life of Sebastián Lerdo de Tejada.* Austin: University of Texas Press, 1951.

Magner, James A. *Men of Mexico.* Milwaukee: The Bruce Publishing Company, 1942.

Mecham, J. Lloyd. *Church and State in Latin America: A History of Politico-Ecclesiastical Relations.* Chapel Hill: University of North Carolina Press, 1934.

Miranda Basurto, Angel. *La Evolución de México.* Mexico: Editorial Herrero, 1959.

Negrete, Doroteo. *La verdad ante la figura militar de Don Miguel Negrete.* Puebla: "La Enseñanza," S.A., 1935.

Ocaranza, Fernando. *Juárez y sus amigos.* 2 vols. Mexico: Editorial Polis, 1939.

Ortega y Pérez Gallardo, Ricardo. *Historia genealógica de las familias más antiguas de México.* 3 vols. Mexico: Imprenta de A. Carranza e Hijos, 1908–1910.

Owsley, Frank L. *King Cotton Diplomacy: Foreign Relations of the Confederate States of America.* Chicago: University of Chicago Press, 1931.

Parra, Porfirio. *Estudio historico-sociológico sobre la reforma en Mexico.* Guadalajara, Imp. de "La Gaceta de Guadalajara," 1906.

Peral, Miguel A. *Diccionario biográfico mexicano.* Mexico: Editorial A.C., no date.

Pérez Verdia, Luis. *Historia particular del estado de Jalisco.* 3 vols. Guadalajara: Tip. de la Escuela de Artes y Oficios del Estado, 1911.

Perkins, Dexter. *The Monroe Doctrine, 1826–1867.* Baltimore: The Johns Hopkins Press, 1933.

Planchet, Regis. *La cuestión religiosa en México ó sea vida de Benito Juárez.* Rome: Desclee, Lefebvre y cía, 1906.

Prida Santacilia, Pablo. *Siguiendo la vida de Juárez.* Mexico: Ediciones Palafox, 1945.

Priestley, Herbert E. *José de Gálvez, Visitor-General of New Spain, 1765–1771.* Berkeley: University of California Press, 1916.

Rivera y Sanromán, Agustín. *Anales mexicanos. La reforma y el segundo imperio.* Lagos: Tip. de V. Veloz., 1890–91.

Roeder, Ralph. *Juárez and His Mexico.* 2 vols. New York: The Viking Press, 1947.

Salado Alvarez, Victoriano. *Episodios nacionales. Santa Anna. La Reforma. La Intervención. El Imperio.* 14 vols. Mexico: Colección Málaga, 1945.

Scholes, Walter V. *Mexican Politics During the Juárez Regime, 1855–1872.* Columbia: University of Missouri Press, 1969.

Smart, Charles A. *Viva Juárez.* New York: J. B. Lippincott Company, 1963.

Teja Zabre, Alfonso. *Historia de México, una moderna interpretación.* 4th ed. Mexico: Ediciones Botas, 1961.

——. *Leandro Valle, un liberal romantico.* Mexico: Imp. Universitaria, 1956.

Untermeyer, Louis. *Forjadores del Mundo Moderno.* Mexico: Biografias Gandesa, 1959.

Valadés, José C. *Don Melchor Ocampo, reformador de México.* México: Editorial Patria, 1954.

——. *El Pensamiento Político de Benito Juárez.* Mexico: Libreria de Manuel Porrúa, n.d.

Villaseñor y Villaseñor Alejandro. *Obras del lic. Alejandro Villaseñor y Villaseñor.* 4 vols. Mexico: Imp. de V. Agüeros, 1897–1910.

Zea Leopoldo. *El positivismo en México.* Mexico: El Colegio de México, 1943.

Articles

Bazant, Jan. "Tres Revoluciones Mexicanos," *Historia Mexicana,* X (October-December, 1960), 220–42.

Berbusse, Edward J. "The Origins of the McLane-Ocampo Treaty of 1859," *The Americas,* XIV (January, 1958), 223–45.

Berry, Charles R. "The Fiction and Fact of the Reform: The Case of the Central District of Oaxaca, 1856–1867," *The Americas,* XXIV (January, 1970), 277–90.

Blumberg, Arnold. "The Mexican Empire and the Vatican, 1863–1867," *The Americas,* XXVIII (July, 1971), 1–19.

Broussard, Ray F. "Vidaurri, Juárez and Comonfort's Return from

Exile," *The Hispanic American Historical Review*, XLIX (May, 1969) , 268–80.

Cadenhead, Jr., Ivie E. "González Ortega and the Presidency of Mexico," *The Hispanic American Historical Review*, XXXII (August, 1952) , 331–46.

Cosío Villegas, Daniel. "La Doctrina Juárez," *Historia Mexicana*, XI (April-June, 1962) , 527–45.

Costeloe, Michael P. "The Mexican Church and the Rebellion of the Polkos," *The Hispanic American Historical Review*, XLVI (May, 1966) , 170–78.

Delmez, Albert J. "The Positivist Philosophy in Mexican Education, 1867–1873," *The Americas*, VI (July, 1949) , 1–12.

Foster, John W. "The Contest for the Laws of Reform in Mexico," *The American Historical Review*, XV (October, 1909-July, 1910) , 526–46.

Cordon, Leonard. "Lincoln and Juárez—A Brief Assessment of Their Relationship," *The Hispanic American Historical Review*, XLVIII (February, 1968) , 75–80.

Hernández Rodríquez, Rosaura. "Comonfort y la intervención francesa," *Historia Mexicana*, XIII (July-September, 1963) , 59–75.

Knapp, Frank L. "The Apocryphal Memoirs of Sebastián Lerdo de Tejada," *The Hispanic American Historical Review*, XXXI (February, 1951) , 145–51.

———. "Parliamentary Government and the Mexican Constitution of 1857," *The Hispanic American Historical Review*, XXXIII (February, 1953) , 65–87.

Knowlton, Robert J. "Some Practical Effects of Clerical Opposition to the Mexican Reform," *The Hispanic American Historical Review*, VL (May, 1965) , 246–56.

Martínez Tamayo, Elena. "Un triangulo político," *Historia Mexicana*, I (July-September, 1951) , 104–13.

Miller, Robert Ryal. "Matías Romero: Mexican Minister to the United States During the Juárez-Maximilian Era," *The Hispanic American Historical Review*, XLV (May, 1965) , 228–45.

Pletcher, David M. "The Building of the Mexican Railway," *The Hispanic American Historical Review*, XXX (February, 1950) , 26–62.

Potash, Robert A. "Historiography of Mexico since 1821," *The Hispanic American Historical Review*, XL (August, 1960) , 383–424.

Raat, William D. "Leopoldo Zea and Mexican Positivism: A Reappraisal," *The Hispanic American Historical Review*, XLVIII (February, 1968) , 1–18.

Robertson, William Spence. "The Tripartite Treaty of London," *The Hispanic American Historical Review,* XX (May, 1940), 167–89.

Scholes, Walter V. "A Revolution Falters: Mexico, 1856–1857," *The Hispanic American Historical Review,* XXXII (February, 1952), 1–21.

————. "Church and State at the Mexican Constitutional Convention, 1856–1857," *The Americas,* IV (October, 1947), 151–74.

————. "*El Mensajero* and the Election of 1871 in Mexico," *The Americas,* V (July, 1948), 61–67.

Index

Acapulco, Guerrero, 42, 43, 53
Aguascalientes (state): supports Juárez, 51; under Governor Chávez, 97
Agustín I. *See* Iturbide, Agustín de
Alamán, Lucas, 39, 41
Alamo, 31
Alatorre, Francisco, 84
Alcabala, 127
Almonte, Juan Nepomuceno: monarchist, 79; returns to Mexico, 87; named president, 88; heads governing board, 92
Alvarado, Dr. Ignacio, 151
Álvarez, Governor Diego: assumes command, 123
Álvarez, Juan: revolts against Gómez Pedraza, 25; and Revolution of Ayutla, 42, 43; interim president, 45; appoints Comonfort, 46; failure to support Juárez, 56
American. *See* United States
Amparo, 120
Aparicio, Francisco: director of Institute of Sciences and Arts, 24
Arista, President Mariano, 38, 39
Arriaga, Ponciano, 40, 43
Arteaga, José Simeón, 32, 51
Assembly of Notables, 92
Austin, Stephen F., 31
Austria, 129
Austro-Prussian War, 109
Auza, Miguel: named to cabinet, 71; suggested by Ortega, 166 n14
Ayuntamiento: of Mexico City, 134, 136, 139, 141

Ayutla: plan of, 42, 43, 160 n45; revolution of, 46, 48, 54
Aztec, 13

Balcárcel, Blas: Secretary of *Fomento*, 119, 168 n60
Bancroft, Hubert H.: cited, 39
Barajas, Bishop Pedro: expelled, 70
Barragán, President Miguel, 31
Barreda, Gabino, 131
Bazaine, Marshal François Achille: named French commander, 95; seeks support, 96; exchange with S. Lerdo, 97; and Vidaurri, 98; and Maximilian, 105, 109; ordered to withdraw, 108; leaves Mexico, 110; defeated at Metz, 130
Benítez, Justo: *porfirista* leader, 136; suspected of desertion, 141
Berriozábal, General Felipe B.: joins Ortega, 64; commands reserve division, 94; resigns, 171 n112
Blancarte, Colonel José María, 39
Bonaparte. *See* Napoleon Bonaparte
Bravo, Nicolás, 42
Britain. *See* Great Britain
Brownsville, Texas, 43
Buchanan, President James, 59, 61
Buena Vista: battle of, 34
Bustamante, President Anastasio: revolts against Guerrero, 26; attempt to overthrow, 29; defeated, 32
Bustamante, Gabino: governor of Federal District, 141

Cabezut, Manuel, 171 n16
Canalizo, General Valentín, 28

[189]